T0261807

Developing iOS Applications with Flex 4.5

Adobe Developer Library

Adobe Developer Library, a copublishing partnership between O'Reilly Media Inc., and Adobe Systems, Inc., is the authoritative resource for developers using Adobe technologies. These comprehensive resources offer learning solutions to help developers create cutting-edge interactive web applications that can reach virtually anyone on any platform.

With top-quality books and innovative online resources covering the latest tools for rich-Internet application development, the *Adobe Developer Library* delivers expert training straight from the source. Topics include ActionScript, Adobe Flex®, Adobe Flash®, and Adobe Acrobat®.

Get the latest news about books, online resources, and more at *http://adobedeveloper library.com*.

Developing iOS Applications with Flex 4.5

Flex 4.5

Rich Tretola

Beijing · Cambridge · Farnham · Köln · Sebastopol · Tokyo

Developing iOS Applications with Flex 4.5
by Rich Tretola

Copyright © 2011 Rich Tretola. All rights reserved.
Printed in the United States of America.

Published by O'Reilly Media, Inc., 1005 Gravenstein Highway North, Sebastopol, CA 95472.

O'Reilly books may be purchased for educational, business, or sales promotional use. Online editions are also available for most titles (*http://my.safaribooksonline.com*). For more information, contact our corporate/institutional sales department: (800) 998-9938 or *corporate@oreilly.com*.

Editor: Mary Treseler	**Cover Designer:** Karen Montgomery
Production Editor: Kristen Borg	**Interior Designer:** David Futato
Proofreader: O'Reilly Production Services	**Illustrator:** Robert Romano

Nutshell Handbook, the Nutshell Handbook logo, and the O'Reilly logo are registered trademarks of O'Reilly Media, Inc. *Developing iOS Applications with Flex 4.5*, the image of a ruff, and related trade dress are trademarks of O'Reilly Media, Inc.

Many of the designations used by manufacturers and sellers to distinguish their products are claimed as trademarks. Where those designations appear in this book, and O'Reilly Media, Inc. was aware of a trademark claim, the designations have been printed in caps or initial caps.

While every precaution has been taken in the preparation of this book, the publisher and authors assume no responsibility for errors or omissions, or for damages resulting from the use of the information contained herein.

ISBN: 978-1-449-30836-0

[LSI]

1313508029

I would like to dedicate this book to our beloved family cats Mickey and Hattrick, who both passed away during the writing of this book. They were both loved very much and will be missed.

Table of Contents

Preface

Introduction to iOS

Apple originally introduced iOS in January of 2007 as the operating system for the iPhone, under the original name of iPhone OS. In June of 2010, Apple renamed its mobile operating system to iOS.

This book will walk you through the creation of your first Adobe AIR application using the Flex 4.5 framework and provide examples of how to interact with the device's components. These include GPS, the camera, the gallery, the accelerometer, the multitouch display, the *StageWebView*, operating system interactions, native components, and more.

Who This Book Is For

Developing iOS Applications with Flex 4.5 is a book targeting all levels of developers. It starts with a basic Hello World application and then quickly moves to more complicated examples where the iOS *APIs* are explored.

Who This Book Is Not For

This book is not for developers who are interested in developing native iOS applications. This book will only provide examples of iOS application development using Adobe Flex 4.5 and ActionScript 3.

Conventions Used in This Book

The following typographical conventions are used in this book:

Menu options
> Menu options are shown using the→character, such as File→Open.

Italic
> Italic indicates new terms, URLs, email addresses, filenames, and file extensions.

Constant width

> This is used for program listings, as well as within paragraphs, to refer to program elements such as variable or function names, databases, data types, environment variables, statements, and keywords.

Constant width bold

> This shows commands or other text that should be typed literally by you.

Constant width italic

> This shows text that should be replaced with user-supplied values or by values determined by context.

This Book's Example Files

You can download the example files for this book from this location:

http://oreilly.com/catalog/9781449308360/

Where necessary, multiple code samples are provided for each recipe to correspond with the different development environments. Each sample will be separated into a folder for the specific environment. Each application should include the needed code for your environment as well as an application descriptor file.

Using the Code Examples

This book is here to help you get your job done. In general, you may use the code in this book in your programs and documentation. You do not need to contact us for permission unless you're reproducing a significant portion of the code. For example, writing a program that uses several chunks of code from this book does not require permission. In addition, answering a question by citing this book and quoting example code does not require permission. However, selling or distributing a CD-ROM of examples from O'Reilly books does require permission. Incorporating a significant amount of example code from this book into your product's documentation does require permission.

We appreciate, but do not require, attribution. An attribution usually includes the title, author, publisher, and ISBN. For example: *"Developing iOS Applications with Flex 4.5* by Rich Tretola (O'Reilly). Copyright 2011 Rich Tretola, 978-1-449-30836-0."

If you think your use of code examples falls outside fair use or the permission given here, feel free to contact us at *permissions@oreilly.com*.

How to Use This Book

Development rarely happens in a vacuum. In today's world, email, Twitter, blog posts, co-workers, friends, and colleagues all play a vital role in helping you solve development problems. Consider this book yet another resource at your disposal to help you solve the development problems you will encounter. The content is arranged in such a way that solutions should be easy to find and easy to understand. However, this book does have a big advantage: it is available anytime of the day or night.

Safari® Books Online

 Safari Books Online is an on-demand digital library that lets you easily search over 7,500 technology and creative reference books and videos to find the answers you need quickly.

With a subscription, you can read any page and watch any video from our library online. Read books on your cell phone and mobile devices. Access new titles before they are available for print, and get exclusive access to manuscripts in development and post feedback for the authors. Copy and paste code samples, organize your favorites, download chapters, bookmark key sections, create notes, print out pages, and benefit from tons of other time-saving features.

O'Reilly Media has uploaded this book to the Safari Books Online service. To have full digital access to this book and others on similar topics from O'Reilly and other publishers, sign up for free at *http://my.safaribooksonline.com*.

How to Contact Us

Please address comments and questions concerning this book to the publisher:

O'Reilly Media, Inc.
1005 Gravenstein Highway North
Sebastopol, CA 95472
800-998-9938 (in the United States or Canada)
707-829-0515 (international or local)
707-829-0104 (fax)

We have a web page for this book, where we list errata, examples, and any additional information. You can access this page at:

http://oreilly.com/catalog/9781449308360/

To comment or ask technical questions about this book, send email to:

bookquestions@oreilly.com

For more information about our books, courses, conferences, and news, see our website at *http://www.oreilly.com*.

Find us on Facebook: *http://facebook.com/oreilly*

Follow us on Twitter: *http://twitter.com/oreillymedia*

Watch us on YouTube: *http://www.youtube.com/oreillymedia*

Acknowledgments

First and foremost, I would like to thank my wife and best friend Kim, as well as my daughters Skye, Coral, and Trinity, for their love and support. I love you all!

I would like to say thanks to the Adobe Flex team and the members of the Flex CAB who provided early access and support to the AIR 2.7 and Flash Builder 4.5 tools and documentation.

Thank you as well to Mary Treseler from O'Reilly for providing this opportunity.

CHAPTER 1

Hello World

This section will walk you through building your first iOS application using Adobe Flash Builder 4.5. If you don't have Flash Builder 4.5, you can get a trial from Adobe at *http://www.adobe.com/products/flashbuilder/*.

Now that you have Flash Builder 4.5 installed, open it and let's get started.

Create a Flex Mobile Project

Create a new Flex Mobile Project by choosing File→New→Flex Mobile Project, as shown in Figure 1-1.

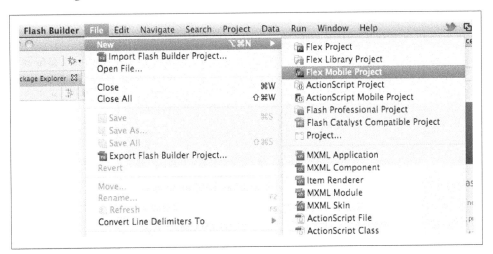

Figure 1-1. Create a Flex Mobile Project

This will open the New Flex Mobile Project wizard, which will walk you through the rest of the project creation process. The first screen you will be presented with will allow you to set the project name, location, and Flex SDK. Enter the name *Hello-World* as the Project name and leave the other settings to their defaults. Click Next, as shown in Figure 1-2.

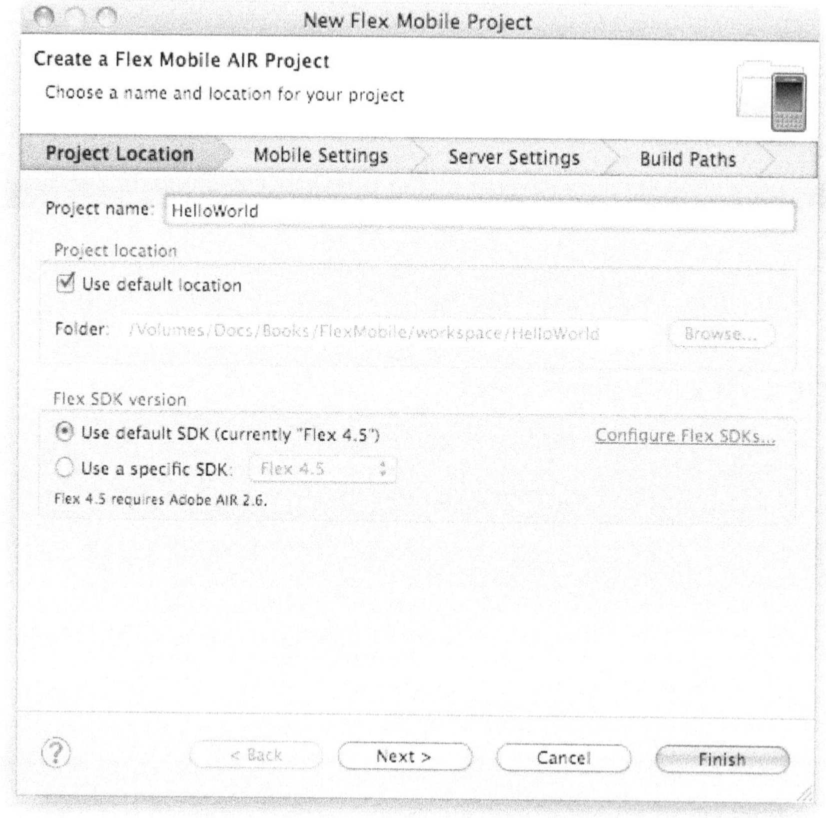

Figure 1-2. Project name and location

The second screen in the new project wizard is where you can select settings specific to the target platform. You will see the options for Apple iOS, BlackBerry Tablet OS, and Google Android. Please select Apple iOS. You also have the option of three different application types, which are Blank, View-Based Application, and Tabbed Application. For this first project, please select View-Based Application, as shown in Figure 1-3, and leave the other settings to their defaults.

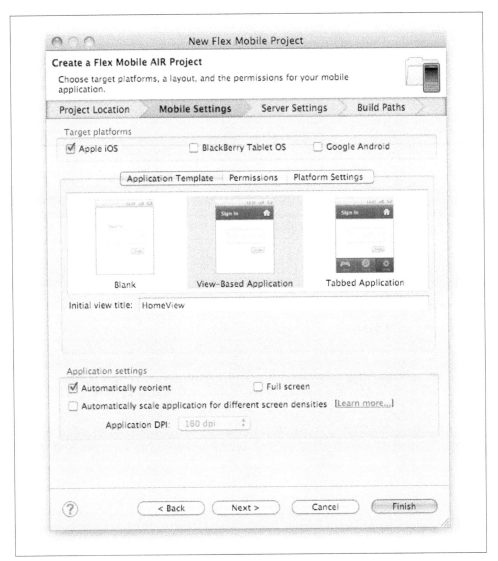

Figure 1-3. Select application template

Next, click on the Platform settings tab. Within this tab, you will be able to select the iOS platform that your application will target. For the purposes of this exercise, leave the Target devices as All, as shown in Figure 1-4. Click Next.

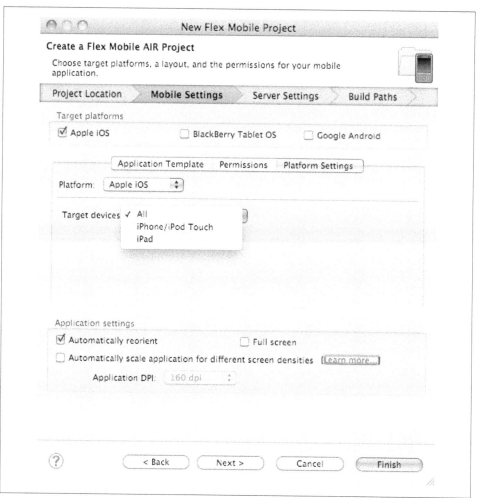

Figure 1-4. Platform settings→Target devices

The next screen allows for the configuration of an application server and output folder. For this project we will not be using an application server, so leave it set to None/Other, and click Next as shown in Figure 1-5.

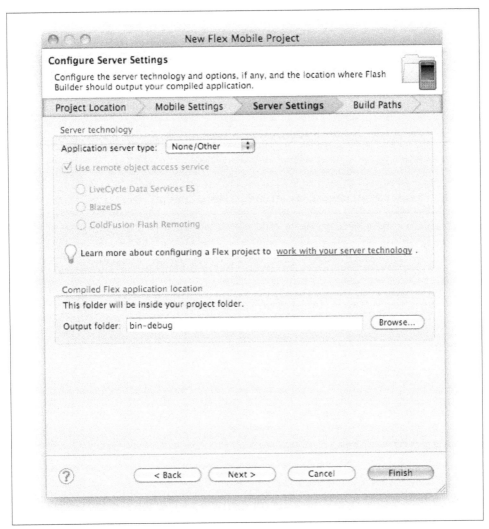

Figure 1-5. Server settings

The last screen that you will see is the Build Paths screen where you will be able to set your Application ID. This setting is very important, as this will identify your application in the App Store. To ensure that your application has a unique identifier, the reverse domain naming convention works best. Figure 1-6 shows the value of *com.domain.mobile.HelloWorld* as the application ID. By replacing the word *domain* with a domain that you own, you can ensure that your application ID is unique. Complete this step and click Finish.

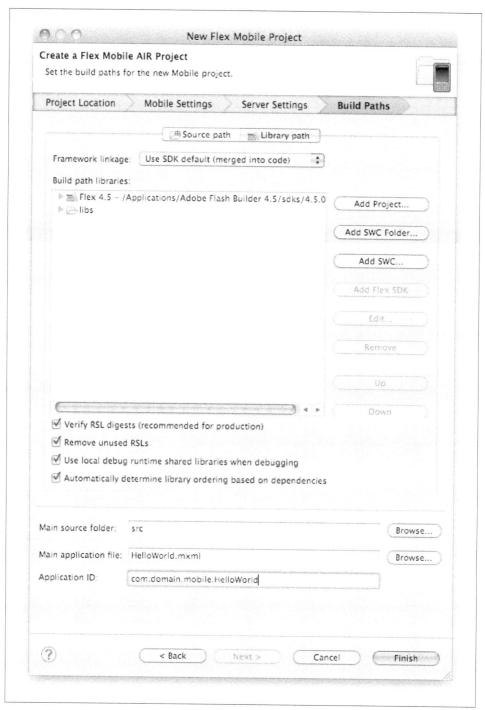

Figure 1-6. Application ID

Flash Builder will now create your new project, and by default the *HelloWorldHome-View.mxml* will be created and opened in the workspace along with the *Hello-World.mxml* main application file. This is shown in Figure 1-7.

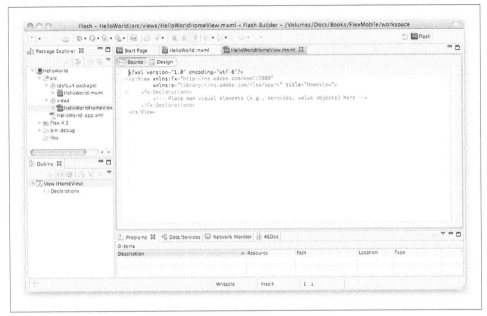

Figure 1-7. A new project has been created

Let's update the contents of the *HelloWorldHomeView.mxml* by adding a Label:

```
<?xml version="1.0" encoding="utf-8"?>
<s:View xmlns:fx="http://ns.adobe.com/mxml/2009"
        xmlns:s="library://ns.adobe.com/flex/spark" title="HomeView">
    <fx:Declarations>
        <!-- Place non-visual elements (e.g., services, value objects) here -->
    </fx:Declarations>

    <s:Label text="Hello World" fontSize="24"
             horizontalCenter="0" verticalCenter="0"/>

</s:View>
```

Before running an application for the first time, you will need to set up either a simulator environment or a device for your testing.

Testing with adl

You can test some basic functionality of your application within Flash Builder using the *adl* simulator—however, for full testing and packaging of your iOS application, you will need to purchase an Apple developer certificate and an Apple device. In this example, I will be using an iPod touch running the latest iOS operating system.

To test with *adl*, simply click on the play button and choose Run As Mobile Application, as shown in Figure 1-8. Next, select Apple iOS as the target platform; and On desktop and Apple iPhone 3GS as the Launch Method, as shown in Figure 1-9. Now click Run and you will see the application running within *adl*, as shown in Figure 1-10.

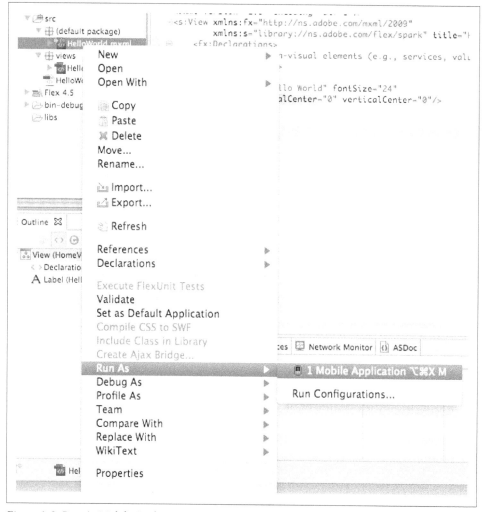

Figure 1-8. Run As Mobile Application

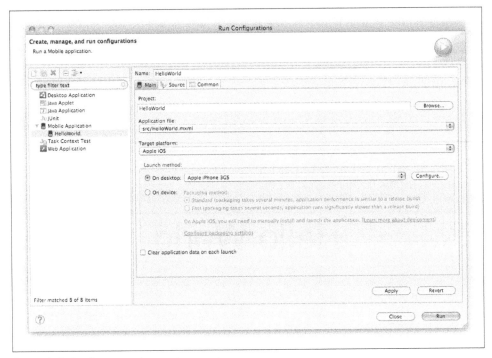

Figure 1-9. Configure runtime environment

Figure 1-10. Running within adl

Preparing to Test on an iOS device

To test on an iOS device, you will first need to purchase a developer certificate from Apple for $99 by visiting *https://developer.apple.com*.

Download and Install Certificate

Once you have your certificate, you can download the *developer_identity.cer* file from the iOS *Provisioning Portal*, as shown in Figure 1-11, and import it. On OSX, you can import into Keychain Access application by double clicking on the *developer_identity.cer* as shown in Figure 1-12. Now, simply right-click on the private key within Keychain Access and export the certificate as a .p12, as shown in Figures 1-13 and 1-14.

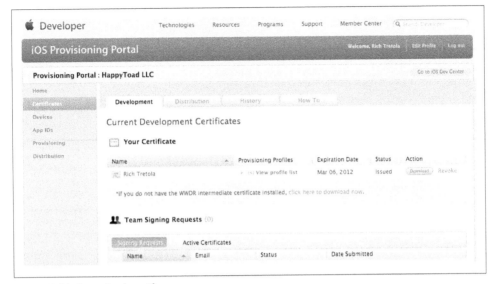

Figure 1-11. Download certificate

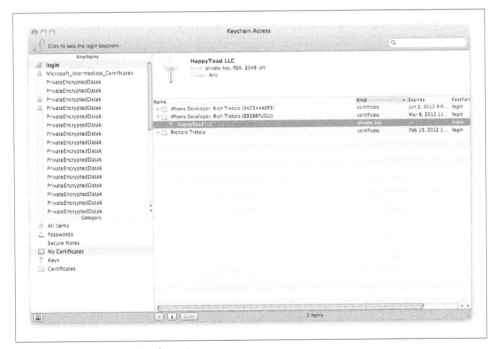

Figure 1-12. Import into Keychain Access

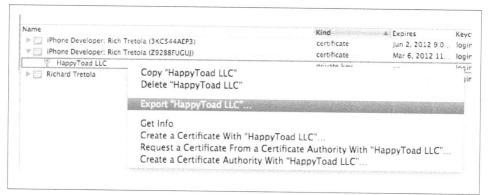

Figure 1-13. Export certificate

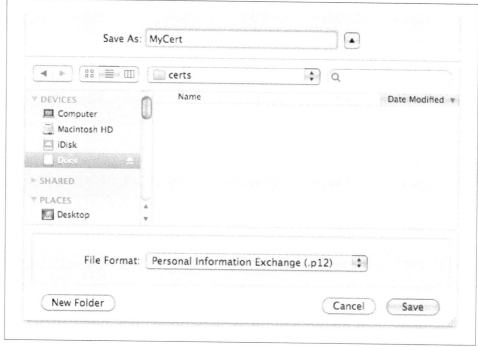

Figure 1-14. Save as a .p12

Add a Device

You will also need to have a device registered with Apple. You can add a device by registering it within the Devices section of the iOS *Provisioning Portal*, as shown in Figure 1-15.

Figure 1-15. Add a device

Create a new App ID

Now that you have a device added, you will need to create a new App ID within the App IDs area of the iOS *Provisioning Portal*. Click on the App IDs menu on the left side of the iOS *Provisioning Portal*, and then click on the New App ID button and complete the form, as shown in Figure 1-16.

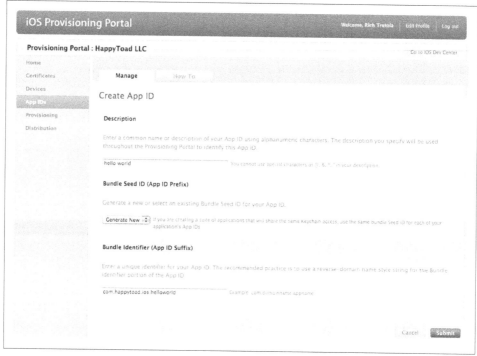

Figure 1-16. Add new App ID

Create a Provisioning Certificate

To create a provisioning certificate, click on the Provisioning link on the left side of the iOS *Provisioning Portal* and then click on the New Profile button. Complete the form and click the Submit button, as shown in Figure 1-17. Next, download the newly created certificate as shown in Figure 1-18 (note that you may need to refresh your browser to get the download button enabled).

Figure 1-17. Create a Provisioning Profile

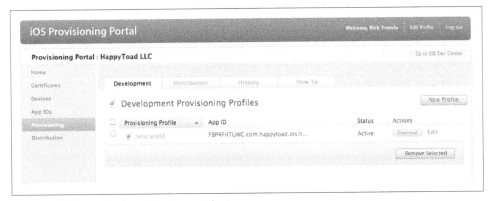

Figure 1-18. Download provisioning certificate

Testing on an iOS device

If you have completed the steps to create a certificate and provisioning certificate, you can now test your application on an iOS device. To do this, right-click on your project name and choose Run As→Run Configurations to open the configuration dialog box, as shown in Figure 1-19. Once the dialog box opens, set the Target Platform as Apple iOS and choose "On device" as the Launch method. You will now need to configure the package settings by clicking on the Configure link, as shown in Figure 1-20, and selecting your *p12* certificate file and *mobileprovisioning* files, as shown in Figure 1-21.

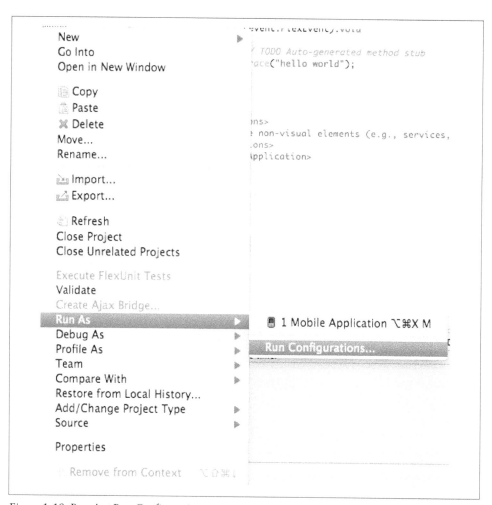

Figure 1-19. Run As→Run Configurations

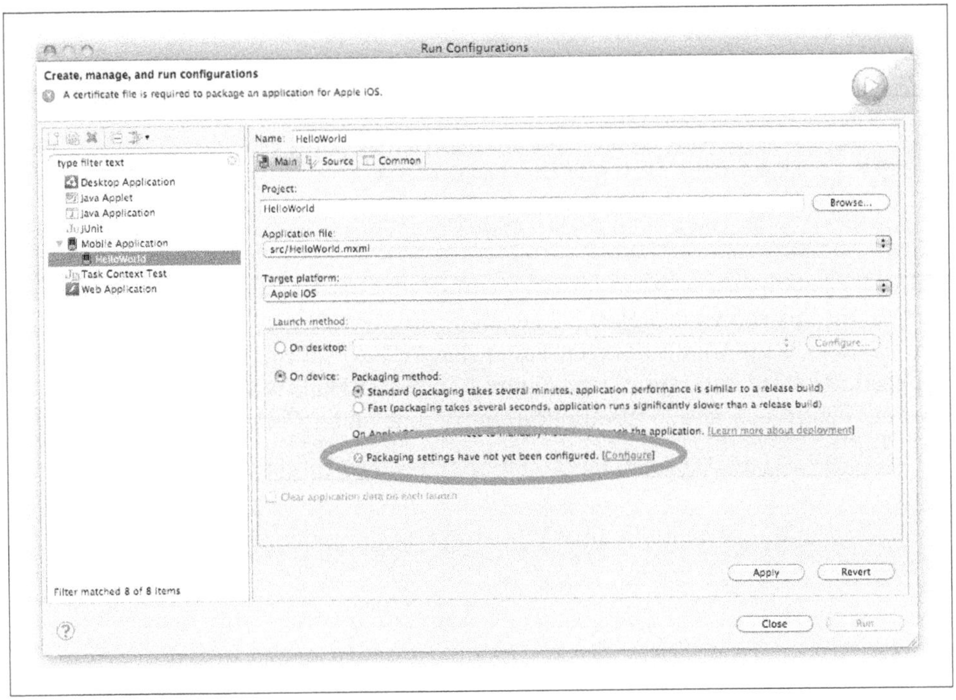

Figure 1-20. The Run Configurations dialog box

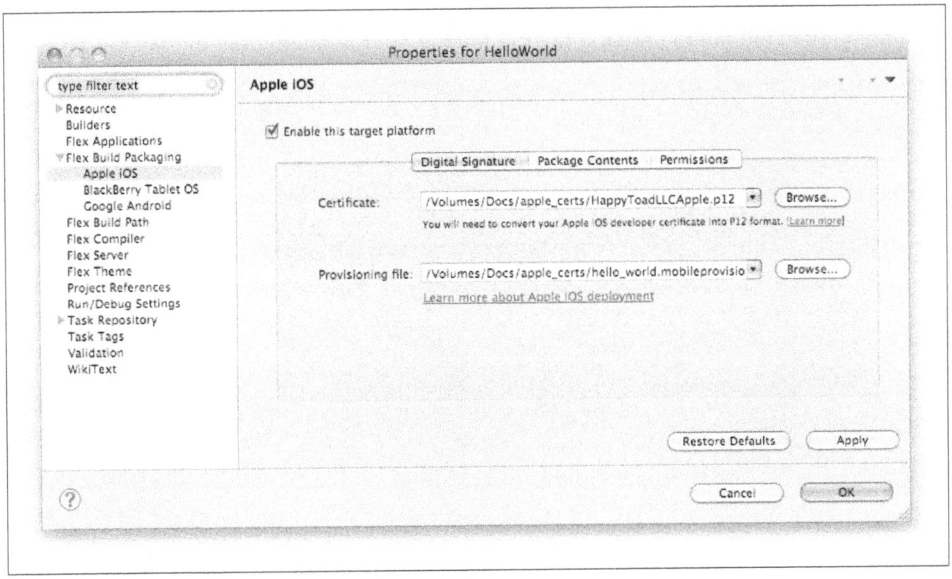

Figure 1-21. Configure certificate and provisioning file

Now that you have your certificates defined, you can click the Run button, which will compile your application to an *.ipa* file for installation on an iOS device.

 Adobe has provided two options for your testing. You can either choose Standard or Fast as your Packaging method.

Figure 1-22 shows the application being compiled. Once the compile has completed, click on the link shown in Figure 1-23 to show the new compiled file and then click on that file to load the application via iTunes. Figure 1-24 shows the HelloWorld-debug application loaded into iTunes, and Figure 1-25 shows HelloWorld-debug installed on an iPod. Figure 1-26 shows the application running on an iPod.

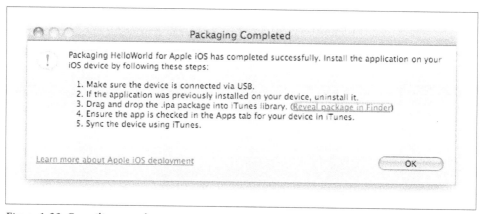

Figure 1-22. Compiling an iOS application

Figure 1-23. Compiling complete

Figure 1-24. HelloWorld-debug loaded into iTunes

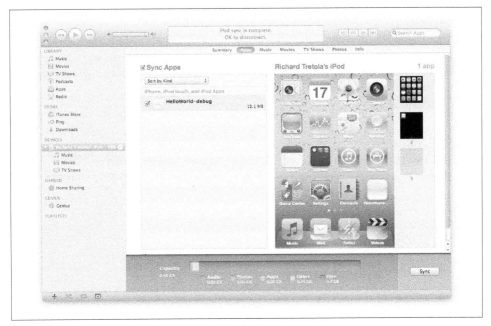

Figure 1-25. HelloWorld-debug installed on iPod

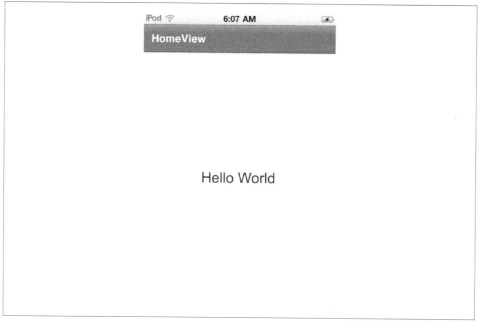

Figure 1-26. HelloWorld-debug running on iPod

Debugging on an iOS device

Now that you have created your Hello World application and run it via the Run Configurations window, you may wish to debug your application. Fortunately for you, the workflow for debugging a Flex Mobile application is the same as debugging any other Adobe Flex or Adobe AIR application.

Update the *HelloWorld.mxml* file to include a *creationComplete* handler as shown below:

```
<?xml version="1.0" encoding="utf-8"?>
<s:ViewNavigatorApplication xmlns:fx="http://ns.adobe.com/mxml/2009"
                            xmlns:s="library://ns.adobe.com/flex/spark"
                            firstView="views.HelloWorldHomeView"

creationComplete="viewnavigatorapplication1_creationCompleteHandler(event)">
    <fx:Script>
        <![CDATA[
            import mx.events.FlexEvent;

            protected function
viewnavigatorapplication1_creationCompleteHandler(event:FlexEvent):void
            {
                // TODO Auto-generated method stub
                trace("hello world");
            }
```

```
    ]]>
  </fx:Script>
  <fx:Declarations>
      <!-- Place non-visual elements (e.g., services, value objects) here -->
  </fx:Declarations>
</s:ViewNavigatorApplication>
```

We will now need to toggle a breakpoint within the application on line 14 to demonstrate a debugging session. To do this, right-click on line 14 within Flash Builder and select Toggle Breakpoint from the context menu. Figure 1-27 shows this process. A small blue dot will appear in the gutter, showing the breakpoint is enabled.

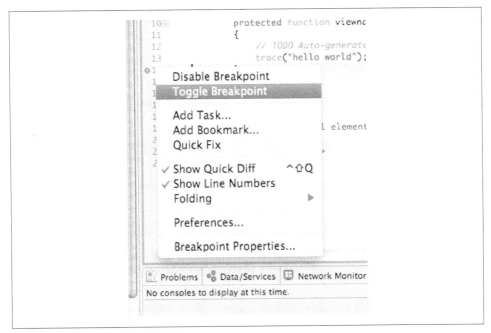

Figure 1-27. Toggle a breakpoint

We are now ready to debug this application. To do this, right-click on the *Hello-World.mxml* file within the Package Explorer and select Debug As→Mobile Application, as shown in Figure 1-28. Since this is the first time debugging this application, the Debug Configurations window will open. To debug this using the Flash builder emulator, select "On device" as the Launch method and select a device from the dropdown menu, as shown in Figure 1-29.

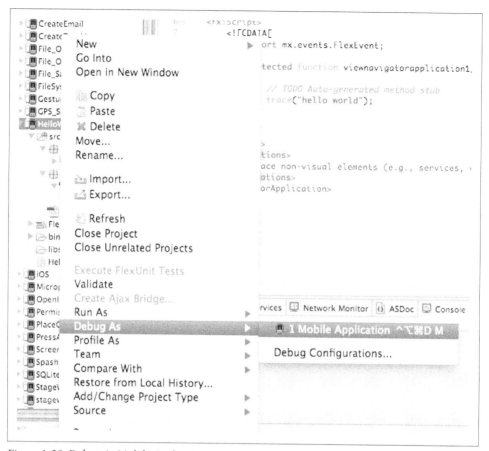

Figure 1-28. Debug As Mobile Application

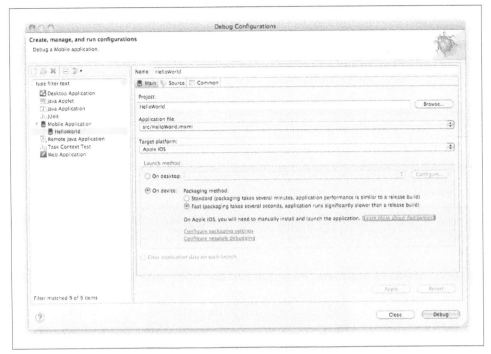

Figure 1-29. The Debug Configurations window

Just as before when you ran your application, your application will compile to an *.ipa* file, which you will need to load to your device via iTunes. Flash Builder will wait while you load the application on the device. Once you have loaded the application and launched it, you will need to enter the IP address of your host machine where Flash Builder is running. See Figures 1-30 and 1-31. Once the application is running, Flash Builder will ask you to switch to the debug perspective.

When asked if you would like to switch to the Flash Builder debug perspective, select "Yes" (see Figure 1-32.) Figure 1-33 shows the application paused on line 14 within Flash Builder's debug perspective. You can see the trace message within the console panel. To allow the application to complete, click the Resume button.

Congratulations, you have just completed your first Flash Builder debug session for an iOS Flex Mobile application.

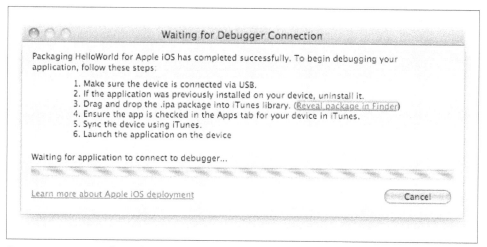

Figure 1-30. Waiting for Debugger Connection window

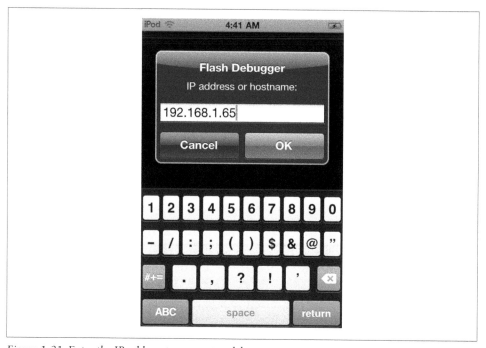

Figure 1-31. Enter the IP address to connect to debugger

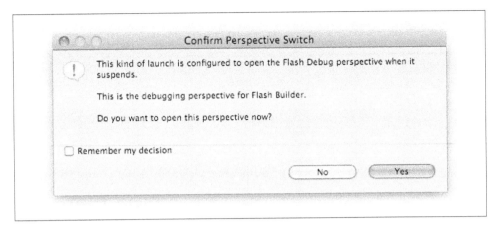

Figure 1-32. Confirming the switch to debug perspective

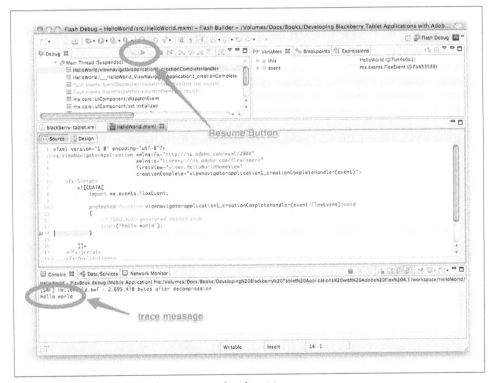

Figure 1-33. Hello World application paused on line 14

CHAPTER 2

Application Layouts

When creating a Flex Mobile project, you have three choices for your layout. They are *Blank Application*, *View-Based Application*, and *Tabbed Application*—and can be seen in Figure 2-1. The selection you make when choosing a layout will determine which files Flash Builder 4.5 will autogenerate. The view-based and tabbed application types come with built-in navigation frameworks. Let's explore each of these.

Blank Application

The blank application layout is best used when you are planning to build your own custom navigation. Choosing this option when creating a new Flex Mobile application within Flash Builder 4.5 will create only the main application file, as shown in the code below:

```
<?xml version="1.0" encoding="utf-8"?>
<s:Application xmlns:fx="http://ns.adobe.com/mxml/2009"
               xmlns:s="library://ns.adobe.com/flex/spark">
    <fx:Declarations>
        <!-- Place non-visual elements (e.g., services, value objects) here -->
    </fx:Declarations>
</s:Application>
```

In the code below I have added a simple Label (you can see the results in Figure 2-2):

```
<?xml version="1.0" encoding="utf-8"?>
<s:Application xmlns:fx="http://ns.adobe.com/mxml/2009"
               xmlns:s="library://ns.adobe.com/flex/spark">
    <fx:Declarations>
        <!-- Place non-visual elements (e.g., services, value objects) here -->
    </fx:Declarations>
    <s:Label text="Blank" fontSize="36"
             horizontalCenter="0" verticalCenter="0"/>
</s:Application>
```

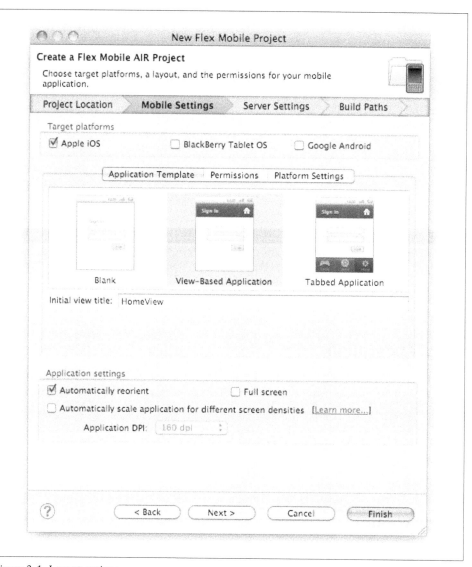

Figure 2-1. Layout options

Figure 2-2. Blank application layout on device

View-Based Application

The view-based application adds the concept of a navigator, which is a built-in navigation framework specifically made for use within mobile applications. The navigator will manage the screens within your application. Creating a new view-based application within Flash Builder 4.5 will result in the generation of two files. These files are the main application file and the default view that will be shown within your application. Unlike the blank application, where the main application file was created with the `<s:Application>` as the parent, a view-based application uses the new `<s:View NavigatorApplication>` as its parent, as shown below:

```
<?xml version="1.0" encoding="utf-8"?>
<s:ViewNavigatorApplication xmlns:fx="http://ns.adobe.com/mxml/2009"
                             xmlns:s="library://ns.adobe.com/flex/spark"
firstView="views.ViewBasedHomeView">
    <fx:Declarations>
        <!-- Place non-visual elements (e.g., services, value objects) here -->
    </fx:Declarations>
</s:ViewNavigatorApplication>
```

The second file that is created is the default view, which is automatically placed in a package named views. In this case it was named *ViewBasedHomeView* was automatically set as the *firstView* property of the *ViewNavigatorApplication*. The autogenerated code for this file is shown below:

```
<?xml version="1.0" encoding="utf-8"?>
<s:View xmlns:fx="http://ns.adobe.com/mxml/2009"
        xmlns:s="library://ns.adobe.com/flex/spark" title="HomeView">
    <fx:Declarations>
        <!-- Place non-visual elements (e.g., services, value objects) here -->
    </fx:Declarations>
    <s:Label text="View-Based" fontSize="48"
             horizontalCenter="0" verticalCenter="0"/>

</s:View>
```

Figure 2-3 shows the view-based application after adding a *Label* to the *ViewBasedHomeView*. As you can see, the navigation framework automatically provides a header and places the title of the current view in that header.

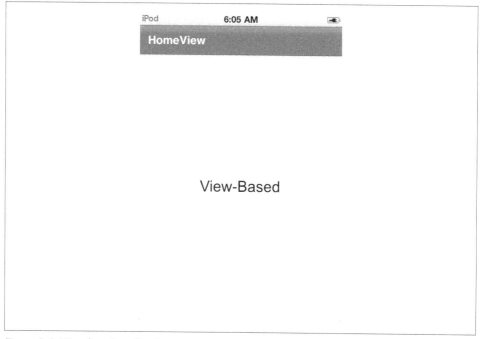

Figure 2-3. View-based application

Now let's explore the navigator a bit. I have created a second view for my application named *SecondView*. I updated the *ViewBasedHomeView* to have a *Button* and also added a *Button* to the *SecondView* shown below. As you can see, each view contains a Button with a similar *clickHandler*. The *clickHandler* simply calls the *pushView* function on the navigator and passes in the view that you wish to have the user navigate to. The Home View will navigate to the Second View, and the Second View will navigate to the Home View. Between each view, a transition is automatically played and the title of the view is reflected in the navigation bar. This can be seen in Figures 2-4 and 2-5:

```
<?xml version="1.0" encoding="utf-8"?>
<s:View xmlns:fx="http://ns.adobe.com/mxml/2009"
        xmlns:s="library://ns.adobe.com/flex/spark" title="HomeView">

    <fx:Script>
        <![CDATA[
            protected function button1_clickHandler(event:MouseEvent):void
            {
                navigator.pushView(views.SecondView);
            }
        ]]>
    </fx:Script>

    <fx:Declarations>
        <!-- Place non-visual elements (e.g., services, value objects) here -->
    </fx:Declarations>

    <s:Button label="Go To Second View"
            horizontalCenter="0" verticalCenter="0"
            click="button1_clickHandler(event)"/>
</s:View>

<?xml version="1.0" encoding="utf-8"?>
<s:View xmlns:fx="http://ns.adobe.com/mxml/2009"
        xmlns:s="library://ns.adobe.com/flex/spark" title="SecondView">

    <fx:Script>
        <![CDATA[
            protected function button1_clickHandler(event:MouseEvent):void
            {
                navigator.pushView(views.ViewBasedHomeView);
            }
        ]]>
    </fx:Script>

    <fx:Declarations>
        <!-- Place non-visual elements (e.g., services, value objects) here -->
    </fx:Declarations>

    <s:Button label="Go To Home View"
            horizontalCenter="0" verticalCenter="0"
            click="button1_clickHandler(event)"/>
</s:View>
```

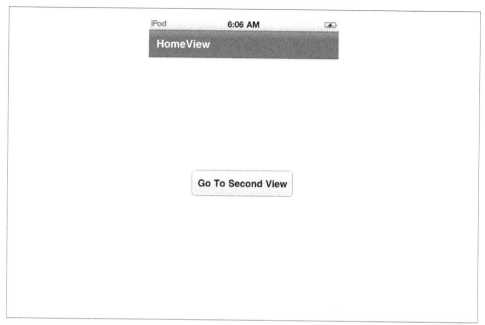

Figure 2-4. HomeView

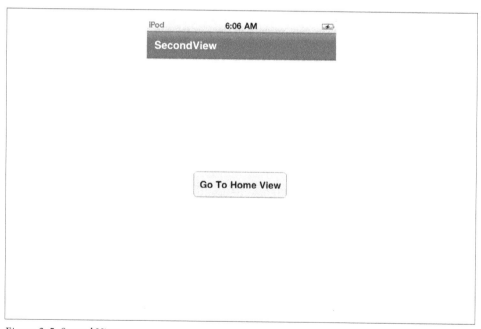

Figure 2-5. Second View

The navigator has additional methods for moving between views within you application. They are as follows:

`navigator.popAll()`

Removes all of the views from the navigator stack. This method changes the display to a blank screen.

`navigator.popToFirstView()`

Removes all views except the bottom view from the navigation stack. The bottom view is the one that was first pushed onto the stack.

`navigator.popView()`

Pops the current view off the navigation stack. The current view is represented by the top view on the stack. The previous view on the stack becomes the current view.

`navigator.pushView()`

Pushes a new view onto the top of the navigation stack. The view pushed onto the stack becomes the current view.

Each of the methods described above allow for a Transition to be passed in. By default they will use a Wipe transition. All pop actions will wipe from left to right, while a push action will wipe from right to left.

Another important item to note about the *navigator.pushView()* is the ability to pass an object into the method call. I have updated the sample below to demonstrate how to use this within your applications.

The *ViewBasedHomeView* shown below now includes a piece of *String* data "Hello from Home View" within the *pushView()* method. The *SecondView* has also been updated to include a new *Label*, which is bound to the data object. This data object is what will hold the value of the object passed in through the *pushView()* method. Figure 2-6 shows the how the *SecondView* is created with the *Label* showing our new message:

```
<?xml version="1.0" encoding="utf-8"?>
<s:View xmlns:fx="http://ns.adobe.com/mxml/2009"
        xmlns:s="library://ns.adobe.com/flex/spark" title="HomeView">

    <fx:Script>
        <![CDATA[
            protected function button1_clickHandler(event:MouseEvent):void
            {
                navigator.pushView(views.SecondView, "Hello from Home View");
            }
        ]]>
    </fx:Script>

    <fx:Declarations>
        <!-- Place non-visual elements (e.g., services, value objects) here -->
    </fx:Declarations>
    <s:Button label="Go To Second View"
              horizontalCenter="0" verticalCenter="0"
              click="button1_clickHandler(event)"/>
</s:View>
```

```
<?xml version="1.0" encoding="utf-8"?>
<s:View xmlns:fx="http://ns.adobe.com/mxml/2009"
        xmlns:s="library://ns.adobe.com/flex/spark" title="SecondView">

    <fx:Script>
        <![CDATA[
            protected function button1_clickHandler(event:MouseEvent):void
            {
                navigator.pushView(views.ViewBasedHomeView);
            }
        ]]>
    </fx:Script>

    <fx:Declarations>
        <!-- Place non-visual elements (e.g., services, value objects) here -->
    </fx:Declarations>
    <s:Label text="{data}" horizontalCenter="0" top="30"/>
    <s:Button label="Go To Home View"
              horizontalCenter="0" verticalCenter="0"
              click="button1_clickHandler(event)"/>
</s:View>
```

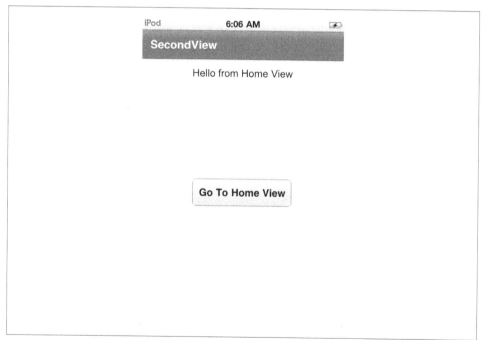

Figure 2-6. pushView() with data passed through

The navigation bar at the top of a view-based application allows you to set specific elements. These are the `navigationContent` and the `actionContent`. By setting these elements, your application can include a common navigation throughout. Here is an example of the view-based application's main file updated with these new elements. You will notice that the navigationContent and actionContent Spark components are defined in MXML. Within each I have included a Button. Each Button has a click Handler that includes a call to one of the navigator methods. The Button that has the label "Home" has a clickHandler, which includes a call to the popToFirstView() method, which will always send the user back to the view that is defined in the first View property of the ViewNavigationApplication. The Button that has the label "Back" has a clickHandler, which includes a call to the popView() method, which will always send the user back to the previous view in the stack. Note that when using popView() you will need to make sure your application is aware of where it is in the stack, as a call to popView() when the user is already on the firstView will send the user to a blank screen. Figure 2-7 shows the application, which now includes the new navigation elements within the navigation bar:

 Although this example utilizes a Button component to demonstrate view navigation, best practices when developing mobile applications would be for your application to rely on the device's native back button navigation.

```
<?xml version="1.0" encoding="utf-8"?>
<s:ViewNavigatorApplication xmlns:fx="http://ns.adobe.com/mxml/2009"
                            xmlns:s="library://ns.adobe.com/flex/spark"
firstView="views.ViewBasedHomeView">

    <fx:Script>
        <![CDATA[
            protected function homeButton_clickHandler(event:MouseEvent):void
            {
                navigator.popToFirstView();
            }

            protected function backButton_clickHandler(event:MouseEvent):void
            {
                navigator.popView();
            }

        ]]>
    </fx:Script>

    <fx:Declarations>
        <!-- Place non-visual elements (e.g., services, value objects) here -->
    </fx:Declarations>

    <s:navigationContent>

        <s:Button id="homeButton" click="homeButton_clickHandler(event)"
                    label="Home"/>

    </s:navigationContent>
```

```
<s:actionContent>
    <s:Button id="backButton" click="backButton_clickHandler(event)"
              label="Back"/>
</s:actionContent>
</s:ViewNavigatorApplication>
```

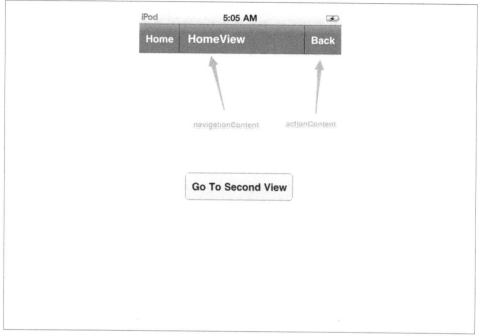

Figure 2-7. navigationContent and actionContent elements

View Life Cycle

The View class includes some new life cycle events specifically added for mobile applications. These events are important for application memory conservation.

- FlexEvent.VIEW_ACTIVATE is dispatched when the view has been activated.

      viewActivate="view1_viewActivateHandler(event)"

- FlexEvent.VIEW_DEACTIVATE is dispatched when the view has been deactivated.

      viewDeactivate="view1_viewDeactivateHandler(event)"

- FlexEvent.REMOVING is dispatched right before FlexEvent.VIEW_DEACTIVATE, when the view is about to be deactivated. Calling preventDefault() will cancel the screen change.

Although this life cycle is great for keeping the application's memory usage minimal, the default behavior to deactivate a view also destroys any data associated with that view. To preserve data so that it will be available if the user returns to that view you can save the data to the `View.data` property.

If you would like to prevent a View from ever being deactivated, you can set the `destructionPolicy` attribute of the View, which normally defaults to `auto` to `never`:

```
destructionPolicy="never"
```

Tabbed Application

The final option for application type is the tabbed application. Selecting *Tabbed Application* (see Figure 2-1) when creating a new Flex Mobile project will trigger Flash Builder to provide some additional functionality. As you can see within Figure 2-8, changing to Tabbed Application allows you to define your tabs right within the new Flex Mobile project interface. In this example, I have added a "My Application" tab and a "My Preferences" tab. After clicking Finish, Flash Builder will create my new tabbed application as well as the tabs I defined as Views. The code example below shows the contents of my main application file, named *Tabbed.mxml*. It is important to note that each of the views I defined (My Application and My Preferences) are included as `ViewNavigator` objects. This means that they will have their own navigator objects and can include their own independent navigation just as we had within the view-based applications we previously discussed. Figure 2-9 shows the running tabbed application. Figure 2-10 shows the view-based application views we previously created within the *My Application* tab of the tabbed application:

```xml
<?xml version="1.0" encoding="utf-8"?>
<s:TabbedViewNavigatorApplication xmlns:fx="http://ns.adobe.com/mxml/2009"
                                  xmlns:s="library://ns.adobe.com/flex/spark">
    <s:ViewNavigator label="My Application" width="100%" height="100%"
firstView="views._MyApplicationView"/>
    <s:ViewNavigator label="My Preferences" width="100%" height="100%"
firstView="views._MyPreferencesView"/>
    <fx:Declarations>
        <!-- Place non-visual elements (e.g., services, value objects) here -->
    </fx:Declarations>
</s:TabbedViewNavigatorApplication>
```

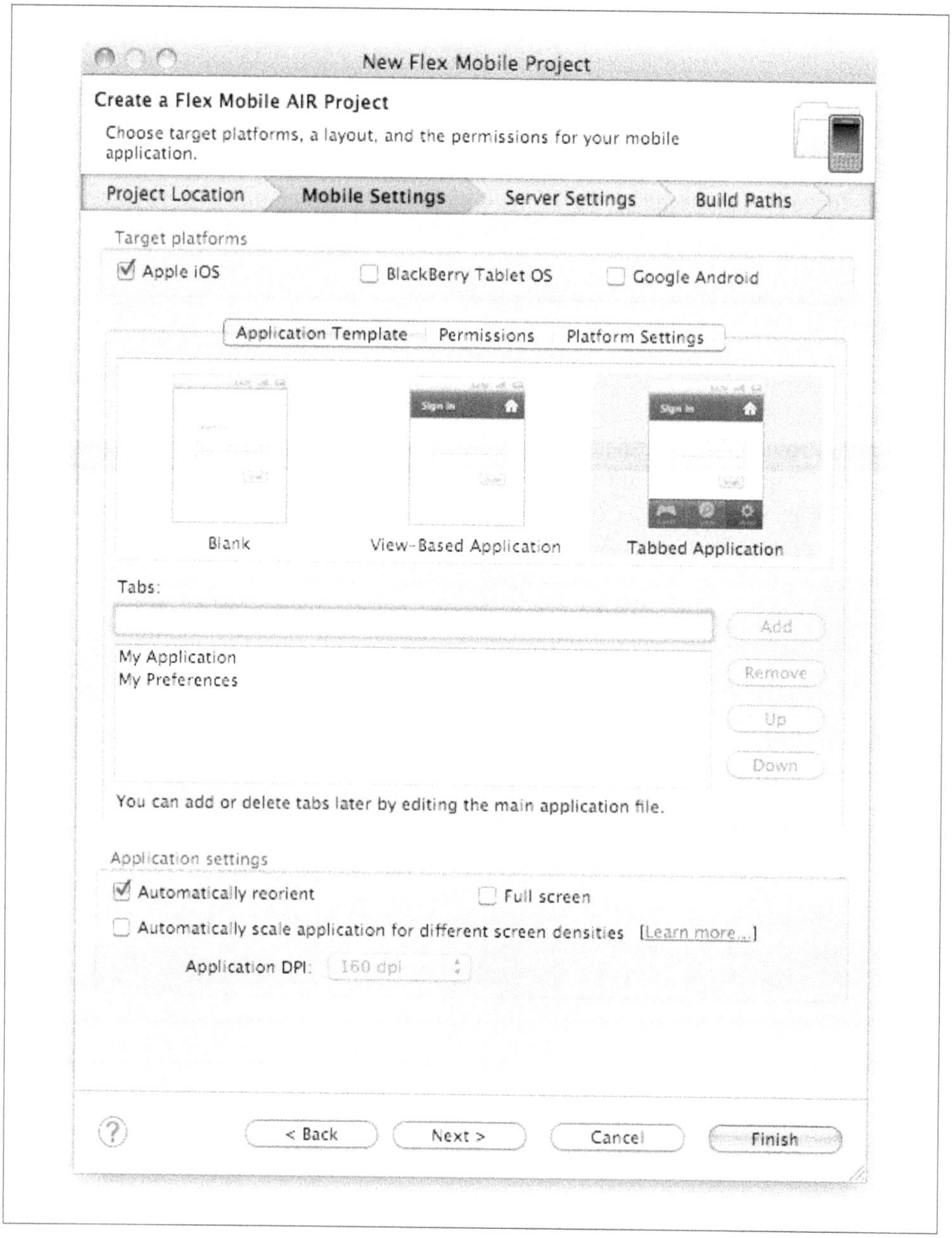

Figure 2-8. Create a new tabbed application

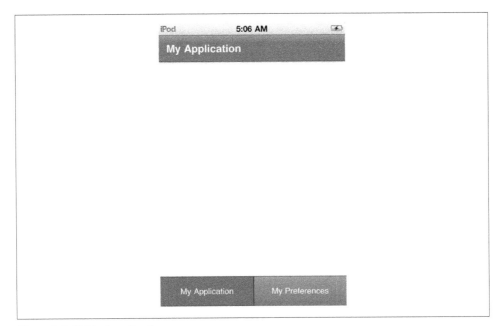

Figure 2-9. Tabbed application

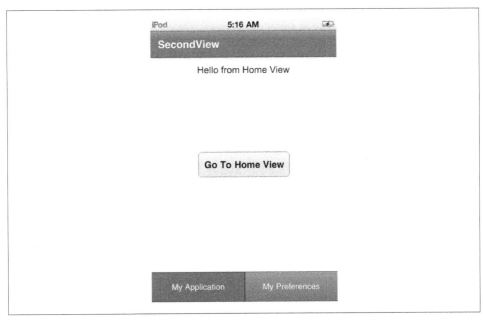

Figure 2-10. Tabbed application with navigators

CHAPTER 3

Configuration Settings

When creating an iOS application, there are several configuration settings available for iOS Flex applications.

Configuration Settings

When creating a new Flex Mobile application, there are a few additional settings that you can configure. These include "Automatically reorient", "Full Screen", and "Automatically scale application for different screen densities". Figure 3-1 shows these options.

Automatically Reorient

This option is set to true automatically, unless you uncheck the box during your project creation. Setting this to true will allow the device to use its accelerometer to automatically switch between portrait and landscape.

This property can be edited at any time within the application's configuration file. This setting can also be changed programmatically while the application is running. See Chapter 5 for more information on this:

```
<autoOrients>false</autoOrients>
```

Full Screen

Checking this box during your project creation will force your application to launch in full screen mode. By default. this is set to false.

This property can be edited at any time within the application's configuration file. This setting can also be changed programmatically while the application is running. See Chapter 5 for more information on this:

```
<fullScreen>false</fullScreen>
```

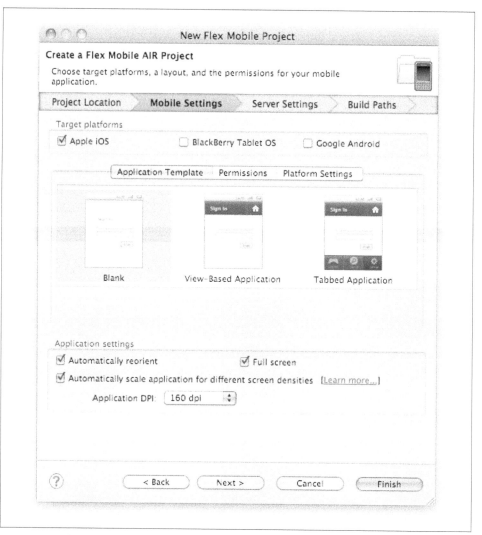

Figure 3-1. Additional configuration settings

Automatically Scale Application for Different Screen Densities

Checking this box will allow your application to automatically scale for different screen densities. It will also allow you to set the default `applicationDPI`, which will be written to the main application file. The options for this value are 160, 240, and 320:

```
<s:Application xmlns:fx="http://ns.adobe.com/mxml/2009"
               xmlns:s="library://ns.adobe.com/flex/spark"
               applicationDPI="320">
```

Aspect Ratio

You have the option to force an application to only run in portrait or landscape mode. Uncommenting the `<aspectRatio>` node within the application's XML configuration file and setting its value to either `landscape` or `portrait` can accomplish this. This setting can also be changed programmatically while the application is running. See Chapter 5 for more information on this:

```
<aspectRatio>landscape</aspectRatio>
```

Additional Configuration Settings

The application descriptor file contains a section specific to iOS with some configuration items that are not covered by Flash Builder's UI. There are several properties that you can set to allow your application to be configured a certain way or only be available for specific devices. A sample is shown below.

Here are the property definitions:

`UIDeviceFamily`
> This node contains an array of strings that represent the different iOS devices. The value of 1 represents *iPhone* and *iPod*, the value of 2 represents *iPad*. So, if you only want your application to be installable on iPad, you would only include `<string>2</string>` within your iPhone descriptors. This is also configurable when you are creating the Flex Mobile application within Flash Builder 4.5. See Chapter 1 for details on creating a new Flex Mobile application.

`UIStatusBarStyle`
> The available options for the `UIStatusBarStyle` are `UIStatusBarStyleDefault` (gray), `UIStatusBarStyleBlackTranslucent` (black with .5 alpha), and `UIStatusBar StyleBlackOpaque` (black). See Figures 3-2 and 3-3.

`UIRequiresPersistentWiFi`
> This setting will force the WiFi connection to stay open throughout the lifetime of your application. If it is set to no (which is the default), it will close after 30 minutes.

`UIApplicationExitsOnSuspend`
> This setting will tell iOS to either suspend your application should run in the background or quit when the user navigates away from it.

`UIRequiredDeviceCapabilities`
> This will block the installation of your application on any iOS device that does not meet the requirements within the array. These options are `microphone`, `gps`, and `camera-flash`.

`requestedDisplayResolution`
> Setting this to high will allow your application to utilize the high-resolution retina displays available on late model iOS devices.

```
<iPhone>
    <InfoAdditions>
        <![CDATA[
            <key>UIDeviceFamily</key>
            <array>
                <string>1</string>
                <string>2</string>
            </array>
            <key>UIStatusBarStyle</key>
            <string>UIStatusBarStyleBlackOpaque</string>
            <key>UIRequiresPersistentWiFi</key>
            <string>YES</string>
            <key>UIApplicationExitsOnSuspend</key>
            <true/>
            <key>UIRequiredDeviceCapabilities</key>
            <array>
                <string>microphone</string>
                <string>gps</string>
                <string>camera-flash</string>
            </array>
        ]]>
    </InfoAdditions>
    <requestedDisplayResolution>high</requestedDisplayResolution>
</iPhone>
```

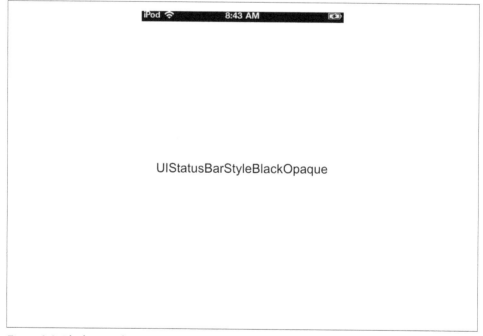

Figure 3-2. Black status bar

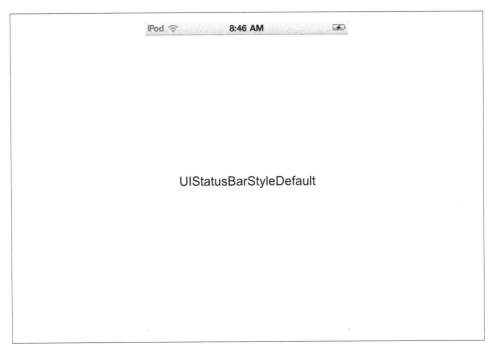

Figure 3-3. Default gray status bar

CHAPTER 4

Exploring the APIs

Now that you know how to create a new application in your choice of layout options and know how to request application permissions, it is time to explore the ways in which your application can interact with the iOS operating system. The AIR 2.7 release includes access to many iOS features. These include the accelerometer, the GPS unit, the camera, the camera roll, the file system, and the multitouch screen.

Accelerometer

The accelerometer is a device that measures the speed or g-forces created when a device accelerates across multiple planes. The faster the device is moved through space, the higher the readings will be across the x, y, and z axes.

Let's review the code below. First, you will notice there is a private variable named `accelerometer` declared of type `flash.sensors.Accelerometer`. Within `application Complete` of the application, an event handler function is called, which first checks to see whether the device has an accelerometer by reading the static property of the `Accelerometer` class. If this property returns as true, a new instance of `Accelerometer` is created and an event listener of type `AccelerometerEvent.UPDATE` is added to handle updates. Upon update, the accelerometer information is read from the event and written to a `TextArea` within the `handleUpdate` function. The results can be seen within Figure 4-1:

```
<?xml version="1.0" encoding="utf-8"?>
<s:Application xmlns:fx="http://ns.adobe.com/mxml/2009"
               xmlns:s="library://ns.adobe.com/flex/spark"
               applicationComplete="application1_applicationCompleteHandler(event)">
    <fx:Script>
        <![CDATA[
            import flash.sensors.Accelerometer;

            import mx.events.FlexEvent;

            private var accelerometer:Accelerometer;

            protected function application1_applicationCompleteHandler
                (event:FlexEvent):void {
                if(Accelerometer.isSupported==true){
                    accelerometer = new Accelerometer();
                    accelerometer.addEventListener(AccelerometerEvent.UPDATE,
                    handleUpdate);
                } else {
                    status.text = "Accelerometer not supported";
                }

            }

            private function handleUpdate(event:AccelerometerEvent):void {
                info.text = "Updated: " + new Date().toTimeString()
                + "\n\n"
                + "acceleration X: " + event.accelerationX + "\n"
                + "acceleration Y: " + event.accelerationY + "\n"
                + "acceleration Z: " + event.accelerationZ;
            }

        ]]>
    </fx:Script>

    <fx:Declarations>
        <!-- Place non-visual elements (e.g., services, value objects) here -->
    </fx:Declarations>
    <s:Label id="status" text="Accelerometer" top="10" width="100%"
        textAlign="center"/>
    <s:TextArea id="info" width="100%" height="220" top="40"
        editable="false"/>
</s:Application>
```

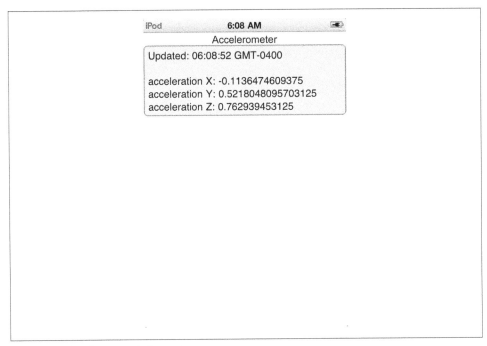

Figure 4-1. Accelerometer information

GPS

GPS stands for Global Positioning System. GPS is a space-based satellite navigation system, which provides reliable location information to your handheld device.

Let's review the code below. First, you will notice there is a private variable named `geoLocation` declared, of type `flash.sensors.GeoLocation`. Within `applicationCom` `plete` of the application, an event handler function is called, which first checks to see whether the device has an available GPS unit by reading the static property of the `GeoLocation` class. If this property returns as true, a new instance of `GeoLocation` is created and the data refresh interval is set to 500 milliseconds (.5 seconds) within the `setRequestedUpdateInterval` method and an event listener of type `GeoLocation` `Event.UPDATE` is added to handle updates. Upon update, the GPS information is read from the event and written to a `TextArea` within the `handleUpdate` function.

Figure 4-2 shows the warning message that iOS will give your user before your application can access the GPS unit. Note: there is also some math being done to convert the speed property into miles per hour and kilometers per hour. The results can be seen within Figure 4-3.

```
<?xml version="1.0" encoding="utf-8"?>
<s:Application xmlns:fx="http://ns.adobe.com/mxml/2009"
               xmlns:s="library://ns.adobe.com/flex/spark"
               applicationComplete="application1_applicationCompleteHandler(event)">
    <fx:Script>
        <![CDATA[
            import mx.events.FlexEvent;

            import flash.sensors.Geolocation;

            private var geoLocation:Geolocation;

            protected function application1_applicationCompleteHandler
                (event:FlexEvent):void {
                if(Geolocation.isSupported==true){
                    geoLocation = new Geolocation();
                    geoLocation.setRequestedUpdateInterval(500);
                    geoLocation.addEventListener(GeolocationEvent.UPDATE,
                        handleLocationRequest);
                } else {
                    status.text = "Geolocation feature not supported";
                }
            }

            private function handleLocationRequest(event:GeolocationEvent):void {
                var mph:Number = event.speed*2.23693629;
                var kph:Number = event.speed*3.6;
                info.text = "Updated: " + new Date().toTimeString() + "\n\n"
                    + "latitude: " + event.latitude.toString() + "\n"
                    + "longitude: " + event.longitude.toString() + "\n"
                    + "altitude: " + event.altitude.toString()  + "\n"
                    + "speed: " + event.speed.toString()  + "\n"
                    + "speed: " + mph.toString()  + " MPH \n"
                    + "speed: " + kph.toString()  + " KPH \n"
                    + "heading: " + event.heading.toString()  + "\n"
                    + "horizontal accuracy: "
                    + event.horizontalAccuracy.toString()  + "\n"
                    + "vertical accuracy: "
                    + event.verticalAccuracy.toString();
            }

        ]]>
    </fx:Script>
    <fx:Declarations>
        <!-- Place non-visual elements (e.g., services, value objects) here -->
    </fx:Declarations>

    <s:Label id="status" text="Geolocation Info" top="10" width="100%"
        textAlign="center"/>
    <s:TextArea id="info" width="100%" top="40" editable="false"/>
</s:Application>
```

Figure 4-2. Requesting GPS access

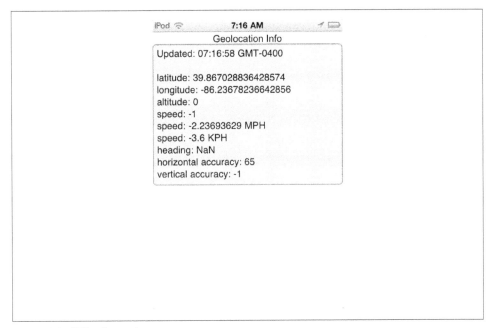

Figure 4-3. GPS information

Camera UI

All recently manufactured full sized iPods, iPhones, and iPads have cameras available. The flash.media.CameraUI class allows your application to utilize the device's native camera interface.

Let's review the code below. First, you will notice there is a private variable named *camera* declared of type flash.media.CameraUI. Within applicationComplete of the application, an event handler function is called, which first checks to see whether the device has an available camera by reading the static property of the CameraUI class. If this property returns as true, a new instance of CameraUI is created and event listeners of type MediaEvent.COMPLETE and ErrorEvent.COMPLETE are added to handle a successfully captured image, as well as any errors that may occur.

A Button with an event listener on the click event is used to allow the application user to launch the CameraUI. When the user clicks the TAKE A PICTURE button, the captureImage method is called, which then opens the camera by calling the launch method and passing in the MediaType.IMAGE static property. At this point the user is redirected from your application to the native camera. Once the user takes a picture and clicks OK, the user is directed back to your application, the MediaEvent.COMPLETE event is triggered, and the onComplete method is called. Within the onComplete method, the event.data property is cast to a flash.Media.MediaPromise object. Since iOS does not automatically write the new image to disk like Android or BlackBerry tablets, we are not able to simply read the file property of the flash.Media.MediaPromise object to display the new image within our application. The solution to this is to load the flash.Media.MediaPromise object into a flash.display.Loader. Within the onComplete method, you will see a new Loader being created and an event listener added to the loader's contentLoaderInfo property to listen for the Event.COMPLETE of the loader. Finally, the loader's loadPromiseFile method is called with the mediaPromise passed in. Once the mediaPromise is loaded, the onMediaPromiseLoaded method is called. The target of the event is cast as a flash.display.LoaderInfo object and its loader property is set as the source of the Image component.

This example also demonstrates how to write the new image to the CameraRoll so that it will persist on the iOS device. Within the onMediaPromiseLoaded method, you will notice that there is a test to see if the application has the permission to write to the CameraRoll, by checking the static property supportsAddBitmapData on the CameraRoll class. In addition, I have added a CheckBox that allows this function to be toggled on and off so that we can easily test to see when images are being written to the Camera Roll. If the supportsAddBitmapData is true and the saveImage CheckBox is checked, a new flash.display.BitmapData object is created using the data from the LoaderInfo and the draw method is called. Finally, a new CameraRoll object is created and the addBitmap Data method is called with the bitmapData passed in.

Utilizing `CameraUI` within your application is different than the raw camera access provided by Adobe AIR on the desktop. Raw camera access is also available within AIR on iOS and works the same as the desktop version.

Figure 4-4 shows the application, Figure 4-5 shows the native camera user interface, and Figure 4-6 shows the application after a picture was taken, the user clicked Use to return to the application, and the new image was loaded. Figure 4-7 shows the new image within the iOS *Photos* application after being written to the `CameraRoll`:

```
<?xml version="1.0" encoding="utf-8"?>
<s:Application xmlns:fx="http://ns.adobe.com/mxml/2009"
               xmlns:s="library://ns.adobe.com/flex/spark"
               applicationComplete="application1_applicationCompleteHandler(event)">
    <fx:Script>
        <![CDATA[
            import mx.events.FlexEvent;
            import mx.graphics.codec.JPEGEncoder;

            private var camera:CameraUI;
            private var loader:Loader;

            protected function
application1_applicationCompleteHandler(event:FlexEvent):void {
                if (CameraUI.isSupported){
                    camera = new CameraUI();
                    status.text="CameraUI supported";
                } else {
                    status.text="CameraUI NOT supported";
                }
            }

            private function captureImage(event:MouseEvent):void {
                camera.addEventListener(MediaEvent.COMPLETE, onComplete);
                camera.addEventListener(ErrorEvent.ERROR, onError);
                camera.launch(MediaType.IMAGE);
            }

            private function onError(event:ErrorEvent):void {
                trace("error has occurred");
            }

            private function onComplete(e:MediaEvent):void {
                camera.removeEventListener(MediaEvent.COMPLETE, onComplete);
                camera.removeEventListener(ErrorEvent.ERROR, onError);
                var mediaPromise:MediaPromise = e.data;
                this.loader = new Loader();
                this.loader.contentLoaderInfo.addEventListener(Event.COMPLETE,
                    onMediaPromiseLoaded);
                this.loader.loadFilePromise(mediaPromise);
            }
```

```
        private function onMediaPromiseLoaded(e:Event):void {
            var loaderInfo:LoaderInfo = e.target as LoaderInfo;
            image.source = loaderInfo.loader;

            if(CameraRoll.supportsAddBitmapData && saveImage.selected){
                var bitmapData:BitmapData = new BitmapData(loaderInfo.width,
                    loaderInfo.height);
                bitmapData.draw(loaderInfo.loader);
                var c:CameraRoll = new CameraRoll();
                c.addBitmapData(bitmapData);
            }
        }

    ]]>
</fx:Script>
<fx:Declarations>
    <!-- Place non-visual elements (e.g., services, value objects) here -->
</fx:Declarations>

<s:Label id="status" text="Click Take a Picture button" top="10" width="100%"
textAlign="center"/>

<s:CheckBox id="saveImage" top="160" label="Save to Camera Roll"
horizontalCenter="0"/>

<s:Button width="350" height="60" label="TAKE A PICTURE"
click="captureImage(event)"
                horizontalCenter="0" enabled="{CameraUI.isSupported}"
                top="80"/>

<s:Image id="image" width="230" height="350" horizontalCenter="0" top="220"/>
</s:Application>
```

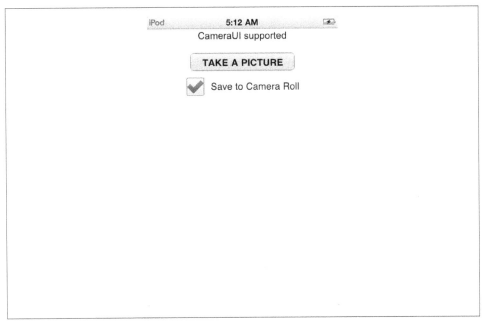

Figure 4-4. Camera UI Application

Figure 4-5. Native Camera UI

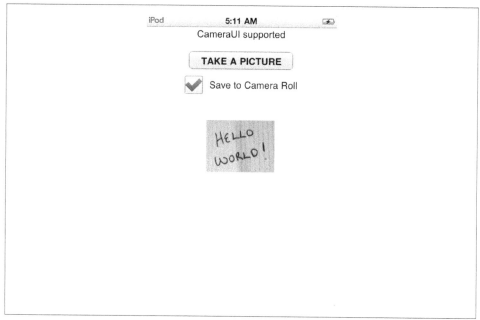

Figure 4-6. Application after taking picture

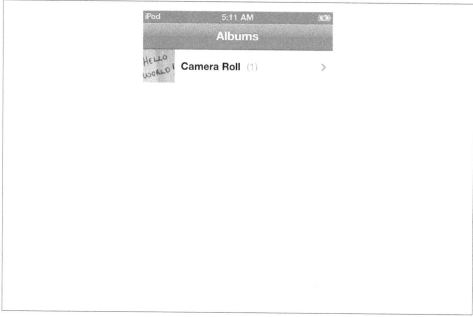

Figure 4-7. iOS Photos application showing an image added to CameraRoll

Camera Roll

The Camera Roll is the access to the camera's gallery of images.

Let's review the code below. First, you will notice there is a private variable named cameraRoll declared of type flash.media.CameraRoll. Within applicationComplete of the application an event handler function is called, which first checks to see if the device supports access to the image gallery by reading the static property of the CameraRoll class. If this property returns as true, a new instance of CameraRoll is created and event listeners of type MediaEvent.COMPLETE and ErrorEvent.COMPLETE are added to handle a successfully captured image as well as any errors that may occur.

A Button with an event listener on the click event is used to allow the application user to allow the user to browse the image gallery. When the user clicks the BROWSE GALLERY button, the browseGallery method is called, which then opens the device's image gallery. At this point the user is redirected from your application to the native gallery application. Once the user selects an image from the gallery, the user is directed back to your application, the MediaEvent.COMPLETE event is triggered and the media Selected method is called. Within the mediaSelected method, the event.data property is cast to a flash.Media.MediaPromise object. Since iOS does not return the file populated on the MediaPromise, we are not able to simply read the file property for display the image within our application like we can with Android or BlackBerry. Instead, the solution is to load the flash.Media.MediaPromise object into a flash.display.Loader. Within the onComplete method, you will see a new Loader being created and an event listener added to the loader's contentLoaderInfo property to listen for the Event.COM PLETE of the loader. Finally, the loader's loadPromiseFile method is called with the mediaPromise passed in. Once the mediaPromise is loaded, the onMediaPromiseLoaded method is called. The target of the event is cast as a flash.display.LoaderInfo object and its loader property is set as the source of the Image component.

Figure 4-8 shows the application and Figure 4-9 shows the application after a picture was selected from the gallery and the user has returned to the application:

```
<?xml version="1.0" encoding="utf-8"?>
<s:Application xmlns:fx="http://ns.adobe.com/mxml/2009"
               xmlns:s="library://ns.adobe.com/flex/spark"
               applicationComplete="application1_applicationCompleteHandler(event)">
    <fx:Script>
        <![CDATA[
            import mx.events.FlexEvent;

            private var cameraRoll:CameraRoll;
            private var loader:Loader;

            protected function
application1_applicationCompleteHandler(event:FlexEvent):void {
                if(CameraRoll.supportsBrowseForImage){
                    cameraRoll = new CameraRoll();
```

```
                    } else{
                        status.text="CameraRoll NOT supported";
                    }
                }

                private function browseGallery(event:MouseEvent):void {
                    cameraRoll.addEventListener(MediaEvent.SELECT, mediaSelected);
                    cameraRoll.addEventListener(ErrorEvent.ERROR, onError);
                    cameraRoll.browseForImage();
                }

                private function onError(event:ErrorEvent):void {
                    trace("error has occurred");
                }

                private function mediaSelected(e:MediaEvent):void {
                    cameraRoll.removeEventListener(MediaEvent.SELECT, mediaSelected);
                    cameraRoll.removeEventListener(ErrorEvent.ERROR, onError);
                    var mediaPromise:MediaPromise = e.data;
                    this.loader = new Loader();
                    this.loader.contentLoaderInfo.addEventListener(Event.COMPLETE,
                        onMediaPromiseLoaded);
                    this.loader.loadFilePromise(mediaPromise);
                }

                private function onMediaPromiseLoaded(e:Event):void {
                    var loaderInfo:LoaderInfo = e.target as LoaderInfo;
                    image.source = loaderInfo.loader;
                }

            ]]>
    </fx:Script>
    <fx:Declarations>
        <!-- Place non-visual elements (e.g., services, value objects) here -->
    </fx:Declarations>

    <s:Label id="status" text="Click Browse Gallery to select image" top="10"
    width="100%" textAlign="center"/>

    <s:Button width="500" height="60" label="BROWSE GALLERY"
    click="browseGallery(event)"
                enabled="{CameraRoll.supportsBrowseForImage}"
                top="80" horizontalCenter="0"/>

    <s:Image id="image" width="230" height="350" top="170" horizontalCenter="0"/>
</s:Application>
```

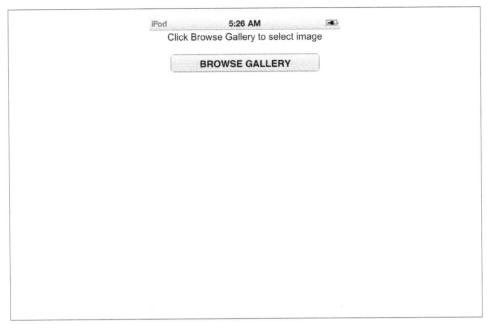

Figure 4-8. Browse Gallery application

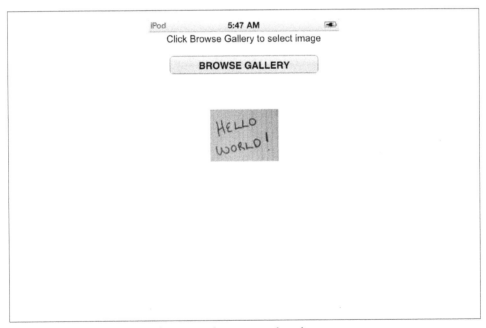

Figure 4-9. Browse Gallery application with a picture selected

Microphone

All recently manufactured full sized iPods, iPhones, and iPads have microphones available.

Let's review the code below. First, you will notice there is a private variable named microphone declared of type flash.media.Microphone. Within applicationComplete of the application an event handler function is called, which first checks to see if the device supports access to the microphone by reading the static property of the Microphone class. If this property returns as true, an instance of the Microphone is retrieved and set to the microphone variable, the *rate* is set to 44, and the setUseEchoSuppression method is used to set the echo suppression to true. There are also variables of type ByteArray and Sound declared within this application. There will be instances of these variables created during use of this application.

There are three button components within the application to trigger the record, stop, and playback functionalities.

Clicking the record button will call the record_clickHandler function, which will create a new instance of the recording variable of type ByteArray. An event listener of type SampleDataEvent.SAMPLE_DATA is added to the microphone, which will call the micData Handler method when it receives data. Within the micDataHandler method, the data is written to the recording ByteArray.

Clicking the stop button will stop the recording by removing the SampleDataEvent .SAMPLE_DATA event listener.

Clicking the play button will call the play_clickHandler method, which first sets the position of the recording ByteArray to 0 so it is ready for playback. It then creates a new instance of the Sound class and sets it to the sound variable. It also adds an event listener of type SampleDataEvent.SAMPLE_DATA that will call the playSound method when it receives data. Finally the play method is called on the sound variable to start the playback.

The playSound method loops through the recording ByteArray in memory and writes those bytes back to the data property of the SampleDataEvent, which then plays through the device's speaker.

To extend this sample, you would need to use some open source classes to convert the recording ByteArray to an *.mp3* or *.wav* file so that it can be saved to disk. The application can be seen in Figure 4-10:

```
<?xml version="1.0" encoding="utf-8"?>
<s:Application xmlns:fx="http://ns.adobe.com/mxml/2009"
               xmlns:s="library://ns.adobe.com/flex/spark"
               applicationComplete="application1_applicationCompleteHandler(event)">
    <fx:Script>
        <![CDATA[
            import mx.events.FlexEvent;
```

```
            private var microphone:Microphone;
            private var recording:ByteArray;
            private var sound:Sound;

            protected function
application1_applicationCompleteHandler(event:FlexEvent):void
            {
                    if(Microphone.isSupported){
                        microphone = Microphone.getMicrophone();
                        microphone.rate = 44;
                        microphone.setUseEchoSuppression(true);
                    } else {
                        status.text="Microphone NOT supported";
                    }
            }

            private function micDataHandler(event:SampleDataEvent):void{
                    recording.writeBytes(event.data);
            }

            protected function record_clickHandler(event:MouseEvent):void
            {
                    recording = new ByteArray();
                    microphone.addEventListener(SampleDataEvent.SAMPLE_DATA,
                        micDataHandler);
            }

            protected function stop_clickHandler(event:MouseEvent):void
            {
                    microphone.removeEventListener(SampleDataEvent.SAMPLE_DATA,
                        micDataHandler);
            }

            protected function play_clickHandler(event:MouseEvent):void
            {
                    recording.position = 0;
                    sound = new Sound();
                    sound.addEventListener(SampleDataEvent.SAMPLE_DATA, playSound);
                    sound.play();
            }

            private function playSound(event:SampleDataEvent):void
            {
                for (var i:int = 0; i < 8192 && recording.bytesAvailable > 0; i++){
                        var sample:Number = recording.readFloat();
                        event.data.writeFloat(sample);
                        event.data.writeFloat(sample);
                }
            }

        ]]>
    </fx:Script>
    <fx:Declarations>
        <!-- Place non-visual elements (e.g., services, value objects) here -->
    </fx:Declarations>
```

```
        <s:Label id="status" text="Click Record to grab some audio, then Stop and Play it
back"
                  top="10" width="100%" textAlign="center"/>
    <s:HGroup top="80" horizontalCenter="0">
        <s:Button id="record" label="Record" click="record_clickHandler(event)" />
        <s:Button id="stop" label="Stop" click="stop_clickHandler(event)" />
        <s:Button id="play" label="Play" click="play_clickHandler(event)" />
    </s:HGroup>
</s:Application>
```

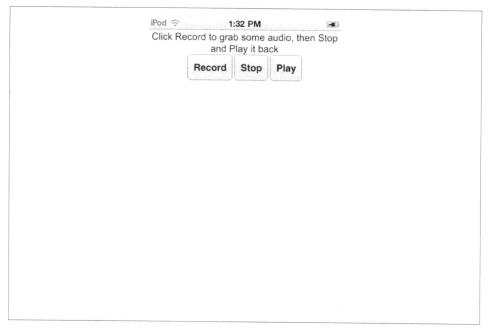

Figure 4-10. Microphone application

Multitouch

One of the navigation methods that are unique to mobile devices is the ability to interact
with an application via gestures on the device's touch screen. Multitouch is defined as
the ability to simultaneously register three or more touch points on the device. Within
Adobe AIR 2.7, there are two event classes used to listen for multitouch events.

GestureEvent

The *GestureEvent* class is used to listen for a two-finger tap on the device. The event
used to listen for this action is the GESTURE_TWO_FINGER_TAP. This event will return the
registration points for the x and y coordinates when a two-finger tap occurs, for both
stage positioning as well as object positioning.

Let's review the code below. Within `applicationComplete` of the application, an event handler function is called which first sets the `Multitouch.inputMode` to `Multitouch InputMode.GESTURE`. Next, it checks to see if the device supports multitouch by reading the static property of the `Multitouch` class. If this property returns as true, an event listener is added to the stage to listen for `GestureEvent.GESTURE_TWO_FINGER_TAP` events. When this event occurs, the `onGestureTwoFingerTap` method is called. The `onGesture TwoFingerTap` method will capture the `localX` and `localY` coordinates, as well as the `stageX` and `stageY` coordinates. If you two-finger tap on an empty portion of the stage, these values will be identical. If you two-finger tap on an object on the stage, the `localX` and `localY` coordinates will be the values within the object, and the `stageX` and `stageY` will be relative to the stage itself. See Figure 4-11 for an example of a two-finger tap on the stage and Figure 4-12 for a two-finger tap on the Adobe AIR image:

```
<?xml version="1.0" encoding="utf-8"?>
<s:Application xmlns:fx="http://ns.adobe.com/mxml/2009"
               xmlns:s="library://ns.adobe.com/flex/spark"
               applicationComplete="application1_applicationCompleteHandler(event)">
    <fx:Script>
        <![CDATA[
            import mx.events.FlexEvent;

            protected function
application1_applicationCompleteHandler(event:FlexEvent):void {
                Multitouch.inputMode = MultitouchInputMode.GESTURE;
                if(Multitouch.supportsGestureEvents){
                    stage.addEventListener(GestureEvent.GESTURE_TWO_FINGER_TAP,
                        onGestureTwoFingerTap);
                } else {
                    status.text="gestures not supported";
                }

            }
            private function onGestureTwoFingerTap(event:GestureEvent):void{
                info.text = "event = " + event.type + "\n" +
                    "localX = " + event.localX + "\n" +
                    "localY = " + event.localY + "\n" +
                    "stageX = " + event.stageX + "\n" +
                    "stageY = " + event.stageY;
            }

        ]]>
    </fx:Script>
    <fx:Declarations>
        <!-- Place non-visual elements (e.g., services, value objects) here -->
    </fx:Declarations>
    <s:Label id="status" text="Do a 2 finger tap both on and off the object"
            top="10" width="100%" textAlign="center"/>
    <s:TextArea id="info" width="100%" top="40" editable="false"/>
    <s:Image width="384" height="384" bottom="10" horizontalCenter="0"
            source="@Embed('adobeair.jpg')"/>
</s:Application>
```

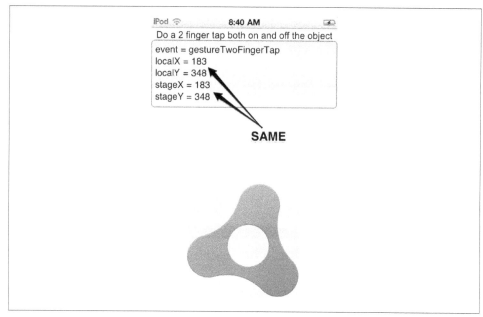

Figure 4-11. Two-finger tap on stage (values are the same)

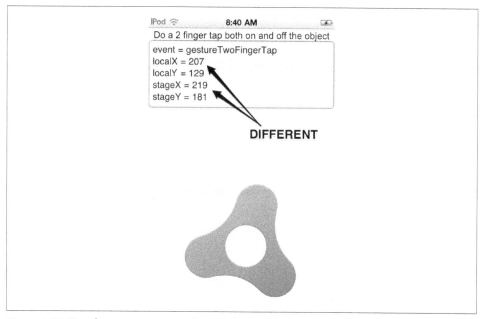

Figure 4-12. Two-finger tap on image object (values are different)

TransformGesture

There are multiple transform gesture events available within AIR 2.7. Each will capture a unique multitouch event. The example below demonstrates how to listen for GESTURE_PAN, GESTURE_ROTATE, GESTURE_SWIPE, and GESTURE_ZOOM events.

Let's review the code below. Within applicationComplete of the application, an event handler function is called which first sets the Multitouch.inputMode to Multitouch InputMode.GESTURE. Next, it checks to see if the device supports multitouch by reading the static property of the Multitouch class. If this property returns as true, event listeners are added to the stage to listen for the TransformGestureEvent.GESTURE_PAN, Transform GestureEvent.GESTURE_ROTATE, TransformGestureEvent.GESTURE_SWIPE, and Transform GestureEvent.GESTURE_ZOOM events.

When a user grabs the object with two fingers and drags the object, the Transform GestureEvent.GESTURE_PAN event is triggered and the onGesturePan method is called. Within the onGesturePan method, the offsetX and offsetY values of this event are written to the text property of the TextArea component. Adding the event's offsetX and offsetY values sets the object's x and y, to move the object across the stage. The results can be seen in Figure 4-13.

When a user grabs the object with two fingers and rotates the object, the Transform GestureEvent.GESTURE_ROTATE event is triggered and the onGestureRotate method is called. Within the onGestureRotate method, the rotation value of this event is written to the text property of the TextArea component. To allow the object to rotate around its center, the object's transformAround method is called and the event's rotation value is added to the object's rotationZ value. The results can be seen in Figure 4-14.

When a user swipes across the object with one finger in any direction, the Transform GestureEvent.GESTURE_SWIPE event is triggered and the onGestureSwipe method is called. Within the onGestureSwipe method, the value of the event's offsetX and offsetY are evaluated to determine which direction the user swiped across the object. This direction is then written to the text property of the TextArea component. The results can be seen in Figure 4-15.

When a user performs a "pinch and zoom" on the object with two fingers, the Trans formGestureEvent.GESTURE_ZOOM event is triggered and the onGestureZoom method is called. Within the onGestureZoom method, the value of the event's scaleX and scaleY written to the text property of the TextArea component. The scaleX value is then used as a multiplier on the object's scaleX and scaleY property to increase or decrease the size of the object as the user pinches or expands two fingers on the object. The results can be seen in Figure 4-16:

```
<?xml version="1.0" encoding="utf-8"?>
<s:Application xmlns:fx="http://ns.adobe.com/mxml/2009"
                xmlns:s="library://ns.adobe.com/flex/spark"
                applicationComplete="application1_applicationCompleteHandler(event)">
```

```
<fx:Script>
    <![CDATA[
        import mx.events.FlexEvent;

        protected function
application1_applicationCompleteHandler(event:FlexEvent):void {
            Multitouch.inputMode = MultitouchInputMode.GESTURE;
            if(Multitouch.supportsGestureEvents){
                image.addEventListener(TransformGestureEvent.GESTURE_PAN,
                    onGesturePan);
                image.addEventListener(TransformGestureEvent.GESTURE_ROTATE,
                    onGestureRotate);
                image.addEventListener(TransformGestureEvent.GESTURE_SWIPE,
                    onGestureSwipe);
                image.addEventListener(TransformGestureEvent.GESTURE_ZOOM,
                    onGestureZoom);
            } else {
                status.text="gestures not supported";
            }
        }

        private function onGesturePan(event:TransformGestureEvent):void{
            info.text = "event = " + event.type + "\n" +
                "offsetX = " + event.offsetX + "\n" +
                "offsetY = " + event.offsetY;
            image.x += event.offsetX;
            image.y += event.offsetY;
        }

        private function onGestureRotate( event : TransformGestureEvent ) : void {
            info.text = "event = " + event.type + "\n" +
                "rotation = " + event.rotation;
            image.transformAround(new Vector3D(image.width/2,image.height/2, 0),
                null,
                new Vector3D(0,0,image.rotationZ
                    + event.rotation));
        }

        private function onGestureSwipe( event : TransformGestureEvent ) : void {
            var direction:String = "";
            if(event.offsetX == 1) direction = "right";
            if(event.offsetX == -1) direction = "left";
            if(event.offsetY == 1) direction = "down";
            if(event.offsetY == -1) direction = "up";
            info.text = "event = " + event.type + "\n" +
                "direction = " + direction;
        }

        private function onGestureZoom( event : TransformGestureEvent ) : void {
            info.text = "event = " + event.type + "\n" +
                "scaleX = " + event.scaleX + "\n" +
                "scaleY = " + event.scaleY;
            image.scaleX = image.scaleY *= event.scaleX;
        }
```

```
            protected function button1_clickHandler(event:MouseEvent):void
            {
                    image.rotation = 0;
                    image.scaleX = 1;
                    image.scaleY = 1;
                    image.x = 40;
                    image.y = 260;
                    info.text = "";
            }

        ]]>
    </fx:Script>
    <fx:Declarations>
            <!-- Place non-visual elements (e.g., services, value objects) here -->
    </fx:Declarations>
    <s:Label id="status" text="Transform Gestures" top="10" width="100%"
            textAlign="center"/>
    <s:HGroup width="100%" top="40" left="5" right="5">
            <s:TextArea id="info" editable="false" width="100%" height="200"/>
            <s:Button label="Reset" click="button1_clickHandler(event)"/>
    </s:HGroup>
    <s:Image id="image" x="40" y="260" width="384" height="384"
                source="@Embed('adobeair.jpg')"/>
</s:Application>
```

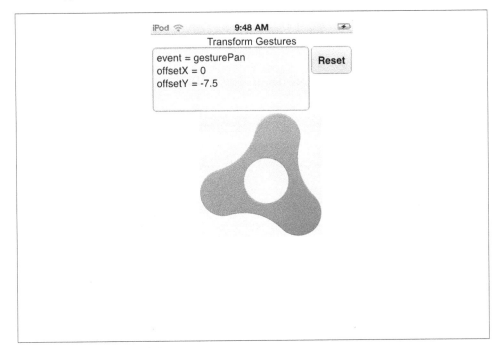

Figure 4-13. GESTURE_PAN event

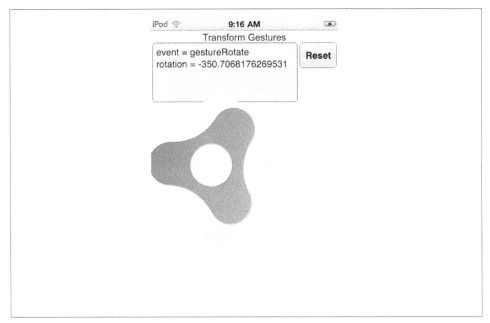

Figure 4-14. GESTURE_ROTATE event

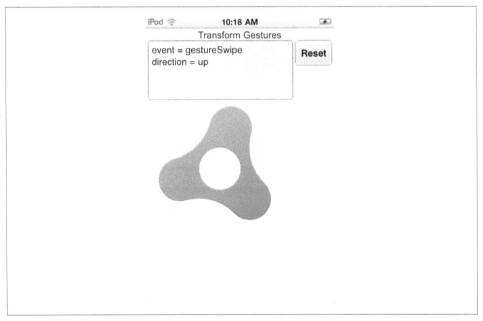

Figure 4-15. GESTURE_SWIPE event

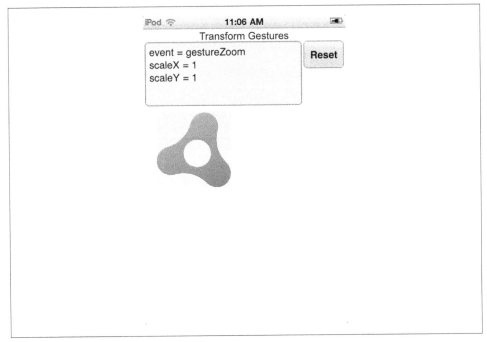

Figure 4-16. GESTURE_ZOOM event

Busy Indicator

A new component has been added to provide feedback to the users within your mobile application. There is no cursor to show busy status as there is in desktop development, so the `BusyIndicator` component was added specifically for this reason. The usage of this component is extremely simple.

Let's review the code below. There is a `CheckBox` with the label "Show Busy Indicator," which when checked, calls the `checkbox1_clickHandler` method. There is a `BusyIndica tor` component with an `id` of `indicator`, with `visible` set to `false`. Within the check box1_clickHandler method, the indicator's `visible` property is set to the value of the `CheckBox`. This simply shows or hides the `BusyIndicator`. Within the `BusyIndicator`, you can set the `height`, `width`, and `symbolColor` to suit the needs and style of your application. The results can be seen in Figure 4-17:

```
<?xml version="1.0" encoding="utf-8"?>
<s:Application xmlns:fx="http://ns.adobe.com/mxml/2009"
               xmlns:s="library://ns.adobe.com/flex/spark">

    <fx:Script>
        <![CDATA[
            protected function checkbox1_clickHandler(event:MouseEvent):void
```

```
            {
                    indicator.visible = event.target.selected;
            }
        ]]>
    </fx:Script>

    <fx:Declarations>
        <!-- Place non-visual elements (e.g., services, value objects) here -->
    </fx:Declarations>

    <s:CheckBox label="Show Busy Indicator"
                horizontalCenter="0"
                click="checkbox1_clickHandler(event)" top="10"/>
    <s:BusyIndicator id="indicator" height="300" width="300"
                verticalCenter="0"
                horizontalCenter="0"
                visible="false"
                symbolColor="black"/>

</s:Application>
```

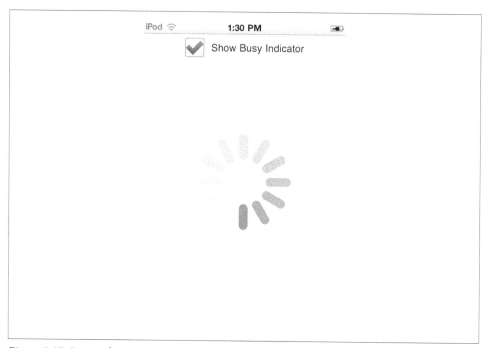

Figure 4-17. Busy Indicator component

CHAPTER 5

Working with the File System

AIR on iOS provides access to the file system to read, write, and update files of all types. This functionality can be very useful not only for reading existing files but also for storing files, media, data, and so on. This chapter will demonstrate how to read and write text files, browse the file system for media files, and create and write to an SQLite database.

File System Access

Just as in the desktop version of Adobe AIR, AIR on iOS provides you access to the file system. The usage is exactly the same.

Folder Aliases

To access the file system you can navigate using several folder static alias properties of the `File` class.

Let's review the code below. On application complete, the `application1_application CompleteHandler` method is called and the static `File` properties are read and written to a `String` variable. This `String` variable is written to the `text` property of a `TextArea` component. Figure 5-1 shows the results:

```
<?xml version="1.0" encoding="utf-8"?>
<s:Application xmlns:fx="http://ns.adobe.com/mxml/2009"
               xmlns:s="library://ns.adobe.com/flex/spark"
               applicationComplete="application1_applicationCompleteHandler(event)">
    <fx:Script>
        <![CDATA[
            import mx.events.FlexEvent;

            protected function
application1_applicationCompleteHandler(event:FlexEvent):void
            {
                var s:String = "";
```

```
                        s += "File.applicationDirectory : "
    + File.applicationDirectory.nativePath + "\n\n";
                        s += "File.applicationStorageDirectory : "
    + File.applicationStorageDirectory.nativePath + "\n\n";
                        s += "File.desktopDirectory: "
    + File.desktopDirectory.nativePath + "\n\n";
                        s += "File.documentsDirectory : "
    + File.documentsDirectory.nativePath + "\n\n";
                        s += "File.userDirectory : "
    + File.userDirectory.nativePath + "\n\n";
                        info.text = s;
                }

            ]]>
    </fx:Script>
    <fx:Declarations>
            <!-- Place non-visual elements (e.g., services, value objects) here -->
    </fx:Declarations>

    <s:Label text="File System Paths" top="10" width="100%" textAlign="center"/>

    <s:TextArea id="info" width="100%" height="100%" top="40" editable="false"/>

</s:Application>
```

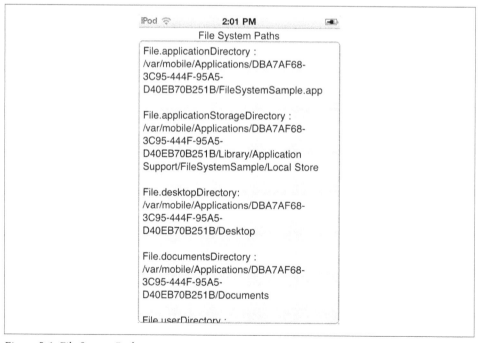

Figure 5-1. File System Paths

Read and Write to the File System

Adobe AIR provides you with the ability to read and write files to the file system. The following example will create a new file and then read it back.

Let's review the code below. There are two TextArea and two Button components that make up this sample. The first TextArea (with the id of contents) will hold the contents of what is to be written to the file, and the second (with the id of results) will output the file contents when read back. The application can be seen in Figure 5-2.

Clicking on the Button with the label of Save will call the button1_clickHandler method. Within the button1_clickHandler method, an instance of File is created with the name *file*, the path is resolved to the userDirectory, and "samples/test.txt" is passed in to the resolvePath method. An instance of FileStream with the name *stream* is created to write the data to the file. The open method is called on the stream object and the file, and FileMode.WRITE is passed in, which will open the file with write permissions. Next, the writeUTFBytes method is called and the contents.text is passed in. Finally, the stream is closed.

Clicking on the Button with the label of Load will call the button2_clickHandler method. Within the button2_clickHandler method, an instance of File is created with the name *file*, the path is resolved to the userDirectory, and "samples/test.txt" is passed in to the resolvePath method. An instance of FileStream with the name *stream* is created to read the data from the file. The open method is called on the stream object and the file, and FileMode.READ is passed in, which will open the file with write permissions. Next, the readUTFBytes method is called, the stream.bytesAvailable is passed in, and the results are set to the results.text property of the second TextArea. Finally, the stream is closed. Figure 5-3 shows the contents of the file within the result's TextArea and the path to the newly created file:

```
<?xml version="1.0" encoding="utf-8"?>
<s:Application xmlns:fx="http://ns.adobe.com/mxml/2009"
               xmlns:s="library://ns.adobe.com/flex/spark">

    <fx:Script>
        <![CDATA[

            protected function button1_clickHandler(event:MouseEvent):void
            {
                var file:File =
File.applicationStorageDirectory.resolvePath("samples/test.txt");
                var stream:FileStream = new FileStream()
                stream.open(file, FileMode.WRITE);
                stream.writeUTFBytes(contents.text);
                stream.close();
            }

            protected function button2_clickHandler(event:MouseEvent):void
            {
```

```
                    var file:File =
File.applicationStorageDirectory.resolvePath("samples/test.txt");
                    var stream:FileStream = new FileStream()
                    stream.open(file, FileMode.READ);
                    results.text = stream.readUTFBytes(stream.bytesAvailable);
                    path.text = "File Path: " + file.url;
                    stream.close();
                }

        ]]>
    </fx:Script>

    <fx:Declarations>
        <!-- Place non-visual elements (e.g., services, value objects) here -->
    </fx:Declarations>

    <s:TextArea id="contents" left="10" right="10" top="10" height="100"/>
    <s:Button right="10" top="120" label="Save" click="button1_clickHandler(event)"/>
    <s:Label id="path" left="10" top="160"/>
    <s:Button left="10" top="200" label="Load" click="button2_clickHandler(event)"/>
    <s:TextArea id="results" left="10" right="10" top="280" height="100"
editable="false"/>
</s:Application>
```

Figure 5-2. File Save application

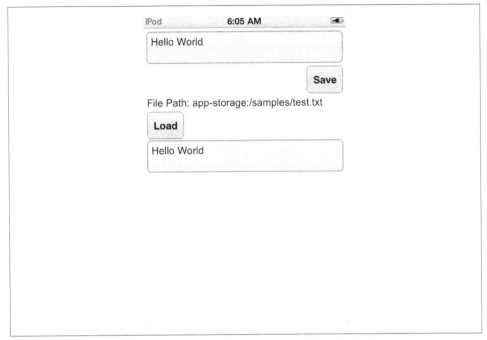

Figure 5-3. File contents loaded into the result's TextArea and file path displayed

SQLite Databases

Just as within Adobe AIR on the desktop, you can utilize an SQLite database for storing data on a mobile device. The example below will create a database, use a simple form to save data to that database, and retrieve and display the stored data.

Let's review the code below. At the top you will see the database file defined as a file called *users.db* within the userDirectory. Next, the SQLConnection is defined. Finally, there are several SQLStatements declared and SQL strings defined, which will be used for working with the database.

Within the applicationComplete event handler, the SQLConnection is initiated and two event listeners are added to listen for SQLEvent.OPEN and SQLErrorEvent.ERROR. Finally, the openAsync method is called and the *db* file is passed in.

After the database is opened, the openHandler function is called. Within this function, the SQLEvent.OPEN event listener is removed. Next, the createTableStmt is created, configured, and executed. This statement will create a new table called *Users* if it doesn't yet exist. If this statement is successful, then the createResult method is called. Within the createResult method, the SQLEvent.RESULT event is removed and the selectUsers method is called.

Within the selectUsers method, the selectStmt is created, configured, and executed. This statement will return all rows within the Users table. This data is then stored within the selectStmt. If this statement is successful, then the selectResult method is called. Within the selectResult method, the data is read from the selectStmt by using the getResults method. It is then cast to an ArrayCollection and set to the dataProvider of a DataGroup, where it is shown on screen by formatting within an itemRenderer named UserRenderer.

All of the processes just described occur as chained events when the application loads up. So if there is any data in the database from previous usage, it will automatically display when the application is loaded. This can be seen in Figure 5-4.

The only remaining functionality is the ability to add a new user. There are two text fields with the ids of firstName and lastName, and a Button that when clicked will call the button1_clickHandler function. Within the button1_clickHandler function, the insertStmt is created, configured, and executed. Notice that within the insertStmt configuration, the parameters firstName and lastName that were defined in the insertSQL method are set to the text properties of the firstName and lastName Text Input components. If this statement is successful, then the insertResult method is called. Within the insertResult method, the selectUsers method is called and the DataGroup is updated, showing the newly added data. This can be seen in Figure 5-5:

Here is the code for the main application:

```
<?xml version="1.0" encoding="utf-8"?>
<s:Application xmlns:fx="http://ns.adobe.com/mxml/2009"
               xmlns:s="library://ns.adobe.com/flex/spark"
               applicationComplete="application1_applicationCompleteHandler(event)">
    <fx:Script>
        <![CDATA[
            import mx.collections.ArrayCollection;
            import mx.events.FlexEvent;

            private var db:File =
File. applicationStorageDirectory.resolvePath("users.db");
            private var conn:SQLConnection;

            private var createTableStmt:SQLStatement;
            private var createTableSQL:String = "CREATE TABLE IF NOT EXISTS User (" +
                                        "userId INTEGER PRIMARY KEY
                                                AUTOINCREMENT," +
                                        "firstName TEXT," + "lastName TEXT)";

            private var selectStmt:SQLStatement;
            private var selectSQL:String = "SELECT * FROM User";

            private var insertStmt:SQLStatement;
            private var insertSQL:String = "INSERT INTO User (firstName, lastName)" +
                                        "VALUES (:firstName, :lastName)";

            protected function
application1_applicationCompleteHandler(event:FlexEvent):void
```

```
{
    conn = new SQLConnection();
    conn.addEventListener(SQLEvent.OPEN, openHandler);
    conn.addEventListener(SQLErrorEvent.ERROR, errorHandler);
    conn.openAsync(db);
}

private function openHandler(event:SQLEvent):void {
    log.text += "Database opened successfully";
    conn.removeEventListener(SQLEvent.OPEN, openHandler);
    createTableStmt = new SQLStatement();
    createTableStmt.sqlConnection = conn;
    createTableStmt.text = createTableSQL;
    createTableStmt.addEventListener(SQLEvent.RESULT, createResult);
    createTableStmt.addEventListener(SQLErrorEvent.ERROR, errorHandler);
    createTableStmt.execute();
}

private function createResult(event:SQLEvent):void {
    log.text += "\nTable created";
    conn.removeEventListener(SQLEvent.RESULT, createResult);
    selectUsers();
}

private function errorHandler(event:SQLErrorEvent):void {
    log.text += "\nError message: " + event.error.message;
    log.text += "\nDetails: " + event.error.details;
}

private function selectUsers():void{
    selectStmt = new SQLStatement();
    selectStmt.sqlConnection = conn;
    selectStmt.text = selectSQL;
    selectStmt.addEventListener(SQLEvent.RESULT, selectResult);
    selectStmt.addEventListener(SQLErrorEvent.ERROR, errorHandler);
    selectStmt.execute();
}

private function selectResult(event:SQLEvent):void {
    log.text += "\nSelect completed";
    var result:SQLResult = selectStmt.getResult();
    users.dataProvider = new ArrayCollection(result.data);
}

protected function button1_clickHandler(event:MouseEvent):void
{
    insertStmt = new SQLStatement();
    insertStmt.sqlConnection = conn;
    insertStmt.text = insertSQL;
    insertStmt.parameters[":firstName"] = firstName.text;
    insertStmt.parameters[":lastName"] = lastName.text;
    insertStmt.addEventListener(SQLEvent.RESULT, insertResult);
    insertStmt.addEventListener(SQLErrorEvent.ERROR, errorHandler);
    insertStmt.execute();
}
```

```
                private function insertResult(event:SQLEvent):void {
                        log.text += "\nInsert completed";
                        selectUsers();
                }

        ]]>
    </fx:Script>
    <fx:Declarations>
            <!-- Place non-visual elements (e.g., services, value objects) here -->
    </fx:Declarations>

    <s:Label text="First name" top="35" left="10"/>
    <s:TextInput id="firstName" left="150" top="10" width="300"/>

    <s:Label text="Last name" top="95" left="10"/>
    <s:TextInput id="lastName" left="150" top="70" width="300"/>

    <s:Button label="Save" click="button1_clickHandler(event)" top="130" left="150"/>

    <s:Scroller height="200" width="100%" left="10" right="10" top="200">
        <s:DataGroup id="users" height="100%" width="95%"
                            itemRenderer="UserRenderer">
            <s:layout>
                    <s:VerticalLayout/>
            </s:layout>
        </s:DataGroup>
    </s:Scroller>

    <s:TextArea id="log" width="100%" bottom="0" height="250"/>

</s:Application>
```

The code for the UserRenderer:

```
<?xml version="1.0" encoding="utf-8"?>
<s:ItemRenderer xmlns:fx="http://ns.adobe.com/mxml/2009"
                        xmlns:s="library://ns.adobe.com/flex/spark">
    <s:Label text="{data.lastName}, {data.firstName}"/>
</s:ItemRenderer>
```

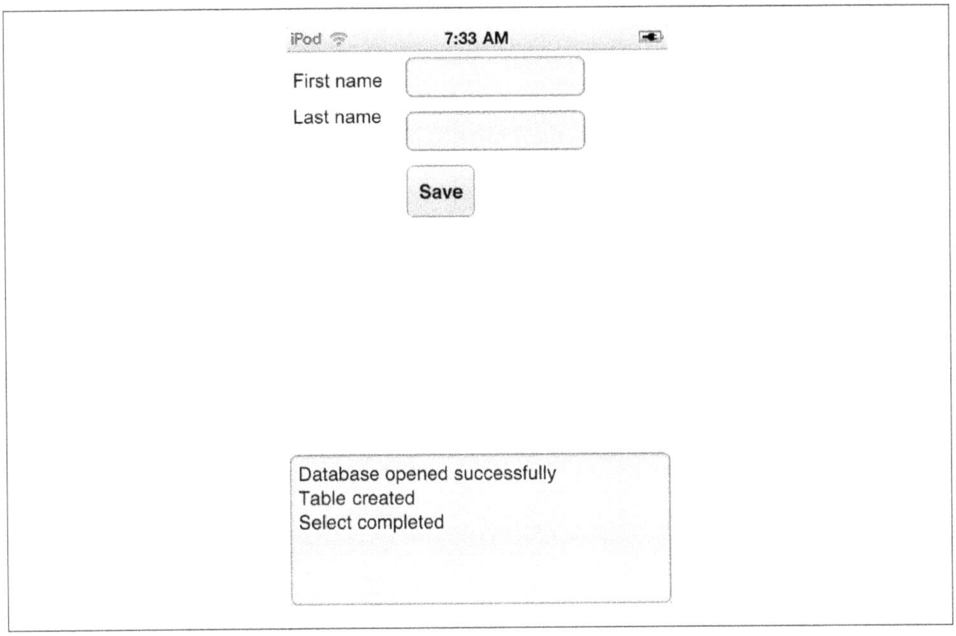

Figure 5-4. SQLite sample application

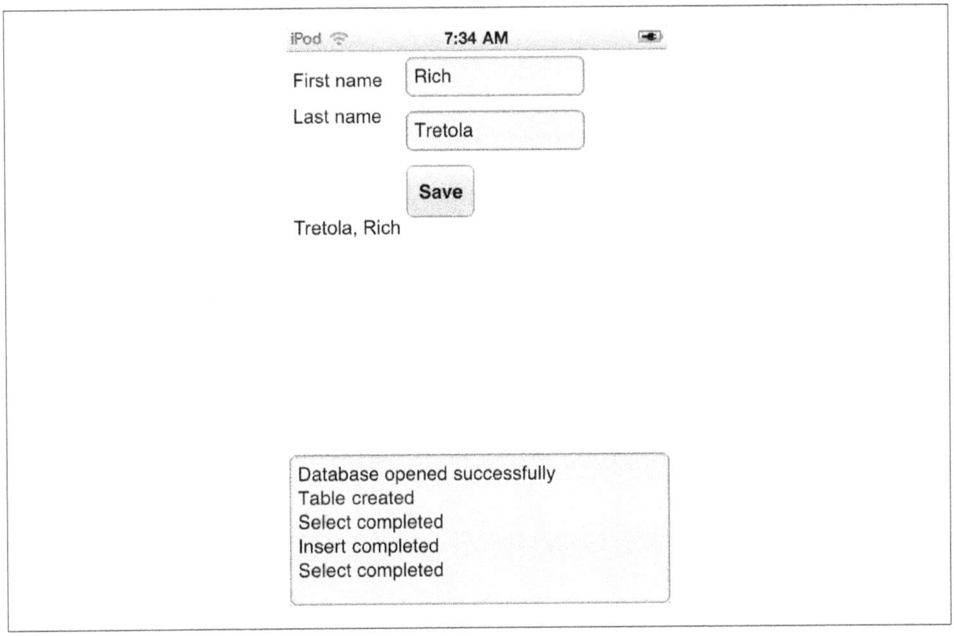

Figure 5-5. After adding a record

CHAPTER 6

OS Interactions

Open in Browser

From within your application, you can open a link using the device's native browser in the same way you can within a traditional browser-based Flex application. This is accomplished with the URLRequest class. Simply creating a new URLRequest and passing this into the navigateToURL method will invoke the user's browser to handle the request. Figure 6-1 shows the sample application running:

```
<?xml version="1.0" encoding="utf-8"?>
<s:Application xmlns:fx="http://ns.adobe.com/mxml/2009"
               xmlns:s="library://ns.adobe.com/flex/spark">

    <fx:Script>
        <![CDATA[
            protected function sendIt_clickHandler(event:MouseEvent):void
            {
                var s:String = "";
                s+= address.text;
                navigateToURL(new URLRequest(s));
            }
        ]]>
    </fx:Script>

    <fx:Declarations>
        <!-- Place non-visual elements (e.g., services, value objects) here -->
    </fx:Declarations>

    <s:Label text="URL" top="40" left="50"/>
    <s:TextInput id="address" top="30" left="160" text="http://www.happytoad.com"
width="400"/>
    <s:Button id="sendIt" label="Open" click="sendIt_clickHandler(event)" top="110"
left="160"/>
</s:Application>
```

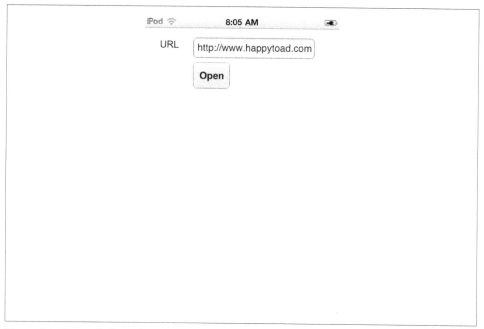

Figure 6-1. Open a link in a browser

Create Text Message

The `URLRequest` class can be used to open the Messages application to send text messages. By prepending the request with *sms:*, iOS will launch the Messages application
when the `navigateToURL` method is called. Figure 6-2 shows the sample application
running and Figure 6-3 shows the Messages application with the phone number prepopulated. Unfortunately, at this time it is not possible to send a message along with
the phone number when opening the Messages application:

```
<?xml version="1.0" encoding="utf-8"?>
<s:Application xmlns:fx="http://ns.adobe.com/mxml/2009"
               xmlns:s="library://ns.adobe.com/flex/spark">

    <fx:Script>
        <![CDATA[
            protected function sendIt_clickHandler(event:MouseEvent):void
            {
                var s:String = "";
                s += "sms:";
                s+= sendTo.text;
                navigateToURL(new URLRequest(s));

            }
        ]]>
    </fx:Script>
```

```
<fx:Declarations>
        <!-- Place non-visual elements (e.g., services, value objects) here -->
</fx:Declarations>

<s:Label text="Send To" top="40" left="50"/>
<s:TextInput id="sendTo" top="30" left="110" text="2125559999" width="200"/>
<s:Button id="sendIt" label="Send" click="sendIt_clickHandler(event)" top="110"
left="110"/>
</s:Application>
```

Figure 6-2. Open a text in the Messages application

Figure 6-3. The Messages application has opened

Create Email

The URLRequest class can be used to open the Messages application to send text messages. By prepending the request with *mailto:*, iOS will launch the Email application when the navigateToURL method is called. There are several properties that can be passed into the URLRequest to set the send-to email address, the email subject, and the email message.

Figure 6-4 shows the sample application running, Figure 6-5 shows the email selection window being launched after the Send button has been clicked, and Figure 6-6 shows the properties being prepopulated in the Gmail application:

```
<?xml version="1.0" encoding="utf-8"?>
<s:Application xmlns:fx="http://ns.adobe.com/mxml/2009"
               xmlns:s="library://ns.adobe.com/flex/spark">

    <fx:Script>
        <![CDATA[
            protected function sendIt_clickHandler(event:MouseEvent):void
            {
                var s:String = "";
                s += "mailto:";
                s+= sendTo.text;
                s+= "?";
                s+= "subject=";
                s+= subject.text;
                s+= "&";
                s+= "body=";
                s+= message.text;
                navigateToURL(new URLRequest(s));

            }
        ]]>
    </fx:Script>

    <fx:Declarations>
        <!-- Place non-visual elements (e.g., services, value objects) here -->
    </fx:Declarations>

    <s:Label text="Send To" top="40" left="50"/>
    <s:TextInput id="sendTo" top="30" left="200" text="rtretola@gmail.com"
        width="300"/>
    <s:Label text="Subject" top="120" left="50"/>
    <s:TextInput id="subject" top="110" left="200" text="hello" width="300"/>
    <s:Label text="Message" top="200" left="50"/>
    <s:TextInput id="message" top="190" left="200" width="300"/>
    <s:Button id="sendIt" label="Send" click="sendIt_clickHandler(event)" top="270"
left="200"/>
</s:Application>
```

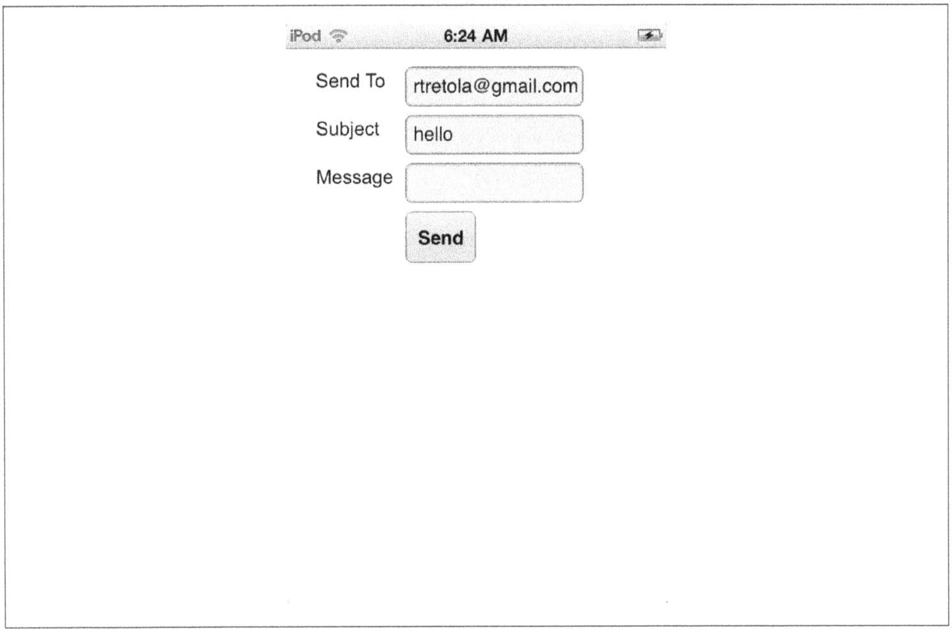

Figure 6-4. Sample email application

Figure 6-5. Email selector that appears after clicking Send

Figure 6-6. Email properties set within Gmail

Place Call

The `URLRequest` class can be used to open the Phone application to place a call. By prepending the request with *tel:*, iOS will launch the Phone application when the `navigateToURL` method is called. Figure 6-7 shows the sample application running and Figure 6-8 shows the Phone application with the phone number prepopulated:

```
<?xml version="1.0" encoding="utf-8"?>
<s:Application xmlns:fx="http://ns.adobe.com/mxml/2009"
               xmlns:s="library://ns.adobe.com/flex/spark">

    <fx:Script>
        <![CDATA[
            protected function sendIt_clickHandler(event:MouseEvent):void
            {
                var s:String = "";
                s += "tel:";
                s+= call.text;
                navigateToURL(new URLRequest(s));


            }
        ]]>
    </fx:Script>
```

```
<fx:Declarations>
        <!-- Place non-visual elements (e.g., services, value objects) here -->
</fx:Declarations>

<s:Label text="Phone #" top="40" left="50"/>
<s:TextInput id="call" top="30" left="160" text="2125559999" width="250"/>
<s:Button id="sendIt" label="Send" click="sendIt_clickHandler(event)" top="110"
left="160"/>
</s:Application>
```

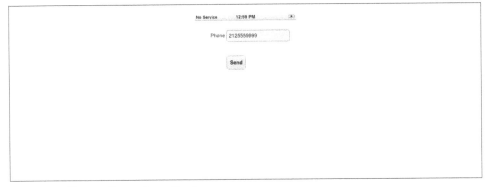

Figure 6-7. Phone call sample application

Figure 6-8. The Phone application attempting to make a call

Splash Screen

Adobe has made it very easy to add a splash screen to your application. A splash screen
is an image that loads first and displays while the application is loading. There are also
several options for the display of this splash screen. Let's look as a basic sample, which
shows the `splashScreenImage` property being set to a *.png* image. Figure 6-9 shows a
splash screen with the default settings:

```
<?xml version="1.0" encoding="utf-8"?>
<s:Application xmlns:fx="http://ns.adobe.com/mxml/2009"
```

```
                xmlns:s="library://ns.adobe.com/flex/spark"
                splashScreenImage="@Embed('happytoad.png')">
    <fx:Declarations>
        <!-- Place non-visual elements (e.g., services, value objects) here -->
    </fx:Declarations>
</s:Application>
```

Figure 6-9. Splash screen with splashScreenScaleMode set to none

There are also some options that can be set on the splash screen. Setting the `splash
ScreenMinimumDisplayTime` and `splashScreenScaleMode` properties on the `Application`,
`ViewNavigatorApplication`, or `TabbedViewNavigatorApplication` tag sets these options.
The example below sets the display time to 3 seconds and the scale mode to `stretch`.

The available options for the `splashScreenScaleMode` property are `letterbox`, `none`,
`stretch`, and `zoom`. Figure 6-10 shows a splash screen with the `splashScreenScaleMode`
set to `stretch`.

```
<?xml version="1.0" encoding="utf-8"?>
<s:Application xmlns:fx="http://ns.adobe.com/mxml/2009"
                xmlns:s="library://ns.adobe.com/flex/spark"
                splashScreenImage="@Embed('happytoad.png')"
                splashScreenMinimumDisplayTime="3000"
                splashScreenScaleMode="stretch">
    <fx:Declarations>
        <!-- Place non-visual elements (e.g., services, value objects) here -->
    </fx:Declarations>
</s:Application>
```

Figure 6-10. Splash screen with splashScreenScaleMode set at stretch

ViewMenu

The `ViewMenu` allows your application to show a menu within your mobile application. By default, this menu will appear at the bottom of your application. `ViewMenu` can only be included within a View class. To create a `ViewMenu`, you will need to define an array of `viewMenuItems`, with each `ViewMenuItem` defined within. The sample below shows an array of `viewMenuItems` with three `ViewMenuItems` defined. There is also a `Button` with a label of Open. The open button click handler will call the `open_clickHandler` function. Within this function, the `ViewMenu` is opened when the `mx.core.FlexGlobals.topLevel Application.viewMenuOpen` is set to true. The `ViewMenu` can be seen in Figure 6-11. There are also click handler functions on each `ViewMenuItem`. The `close_ClickHandler` is called when the close `ViewMenuItem` is clicked. Within the `close_ClickHandler` function, setting the `mx.core.FlexGlobals.topLevelApplication.viewMenuOpen` to false closes the `ViewMenu`:

```
<?xml version="1.0" encoding="utf-8"?>
<s:View xmlns:fx="http://ns.adobe.com/mxml/2009"
        xmlns:s="library://ns.adobe.com/flex/spark" title="HomeView">

    <fx:Script>
        <![CDATA[
            protected function open_clickHandler(event:MouseEvent):void
```

```
                {
                        mx.core.FlexGlobals.topLevelApplication.viewMenuOpen=true;
                }

                protected function newContact_clickHandler(event:MouseEvent):void
                {
                        // TODO Auto-generated method stub

                }

                protected function search_clickHandler(event:MouseEvent):void
                {
                        // TODO Auto-generated method stub

                }

                protected function close_clickHandler(event:MouseEvent):void
                {
                        mx.core.FlexGlobals.topLevelApplication.viewMenuOpen=false;
                }

        ]]>
    </fx:Script>

    <fx:Declarations>
        <!-- Place non-visual elements (e.g., services, value objects) here -->
    </fx:Declarations>
    <s:viewMenuItems>
        <s:ViewMenuItem label="Search" id="search"
                          click="search_clickHandler(event)"/>
        <s:ViewMenuItem label="New Contact" id="newContact"
                          click="newContact_clickHandler(event)"/>
        <s:ViewMenuItem label="Close" id="close"
                          click="close_clickHandler(event)"/>
    </s:viewMenuItems>
    <s:Button label="Open Menu" id="open"
                 horizontalCenter="0" verticalCenter="0"
                 click="open_clickHandler(event)"/>
</s:View>
```

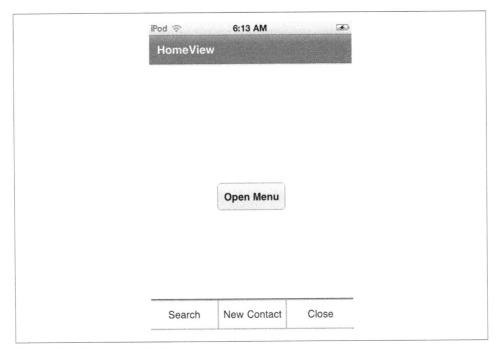

Figure 6-11. ViewMenu with 3 items

StageWebView

The StageWebView allows for web (HTML and Flash on supported devices) and video content to be loaded into a Flex application. StageWebView will utilize the native browser to load HTML into your application.

Let's review the code below. First, you will notice there is a private variable named stageWebView declared of type flash.media.StageWebView. Within applicationCom plete of the application, an event handler function is called, which first checks to see if the device supports StageWebView by reading the static property of the StageWebView class. If this property returns as true, a new instance of StageWebView is created, then a new Rectangle is created, sized to fill the remaining screen and set to the viewport property of the stageWebView.

There is a TextInput component with the id of urlAddress, which holds the address that will be shown in the StageWebView and a Button with the label GO.

Clicking on the GO button will call the button1_clickHandler method. Within the button1_clickHandler method, the loadURL method is called with the urlAddress .text property passed in. This triggers the StageWebView to load the URL.

The results can be seen within Figure 6-12:

```xml
<?xml version="1.0" encoding="utf-8"?>
<s:Application xmlns:fx="http://ns.adobe.com/mxml/2009"
               xmlns:s="library://ns.adobe.com/flex/spark"
               applicationComplete="application1_applicationCompleteHandler(event)">
    <fx:Script>
        <![CDATA[
            import mx.events.FlexEvent;

            private var stageWebView:StageWebView;
            private var rect:Rectangle;

            protected function
application1_applicationCompleteHandler(event:FlexEvent):void
            {
                if(StageWebView.isSupported==true){
                    stageWebView = new StageWebView();
                    stageWebView.viewPort =
new Rectangle(5,80,stage.width-10,stage.height-90);
                    stageWebView.stage = this.stage;
                } else {
                    urlAddress.text = "StageWebView not supported";
                }
            }

            protected function button1_clickHandler(event:MouseEvent):void
            {
                stageWebView.loadURL(urlAddress.text);
            }

        ]]>
    </fx:Script>
    <fx:Declarations>
        <!-- Place non-visual elements (e.g., services, value objects) here -->
    </fx:Declarations>

    <s:TextInput id="urlAddress" left="5" right="80" top="15"
text="http://www.google.com"/>
    <s:Button right="5" top="5" label="GO" click="button1_clickHandler(event)"/>

</s:Application>
```

Figure 6-12. StageWebView with Google.com loaded

Screen Options

There are several options available to programmatically control several areas of the screen layout. These options include the layout of the application, whether or not to show the action bar in a view-based or tabbed application, and whether or not to show the application in full screen mode. This sample application can be seen in Figure 6-13.

Layout

The options for your application layout are portrait (where the application shows vertically in the device), or landscape (where the application appears horizontally). Setting the aspect ratio by calling the `setAspectRatio` method on the `stage` can change the application's layout. The `StageAspectRatio` class contains two static values that should be used to set the aspect ratio.

The code below includes a RadioGroup with the id of orientation. There are two RadioButton components in this group with values of portrait and landscape. When clicking on one of these radio buttons, the radiobutton1_clickHandler method is called. Within this method, the orientation.selectedValue is tested.

If orientation.selectedValue is equal to portrait, the stage.setAspectRatio method is called and StageAspectRatio.PORTRAIT is passed in. If orientation.selectedValue is equal to landscape, the stage.setAspectRatio method is called and StageAspectRatio.LANDSCAPE is passed in. The results can be seen in Figure 6-14.

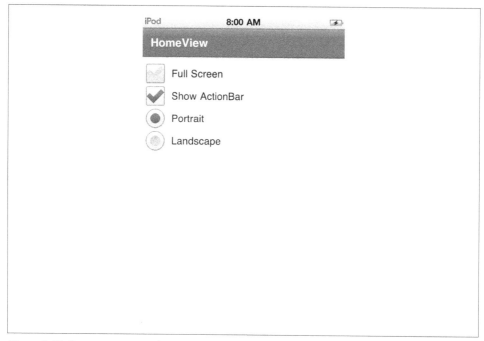

Figure 6-13. Screen options application

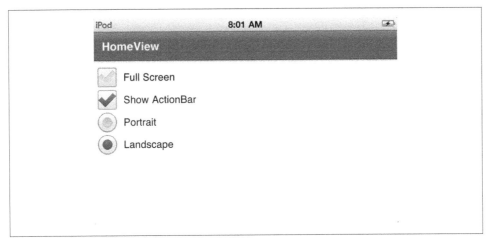

Figure 6-14. Landscape mode

Full Screen

Utilizing the entire screen for your mobile application is an option that you can set within your application, and there are a few choices when this change is requested. To put an application in full screen mode, you will need to set the displayState property on the stage. There are several static properties within the StageDisplayState class that can be used for this.

The code below includes a CheckBox with the label "Full Screen". This CheckBox is set to non-selected by default, as that is the normal state of the application. When clicking on this CheckBox to check or uncheck the value, the checkbox1_clickHandler is called. If the checkbox is selected, the stage.displayState is set to StageDisplayState .FULL_SCREEN_INTERACTIVE. If the checkbox is unselected, the stage.displayState is set to StageDisplayState.NORMAL. Note that the StageDisplayState also has a static property of StageDisplayState.FULL_SCREEN. This property can be used to put the application in full screen mode when the keyboard is unnecessary. The results can be seen in Figure 6-15.

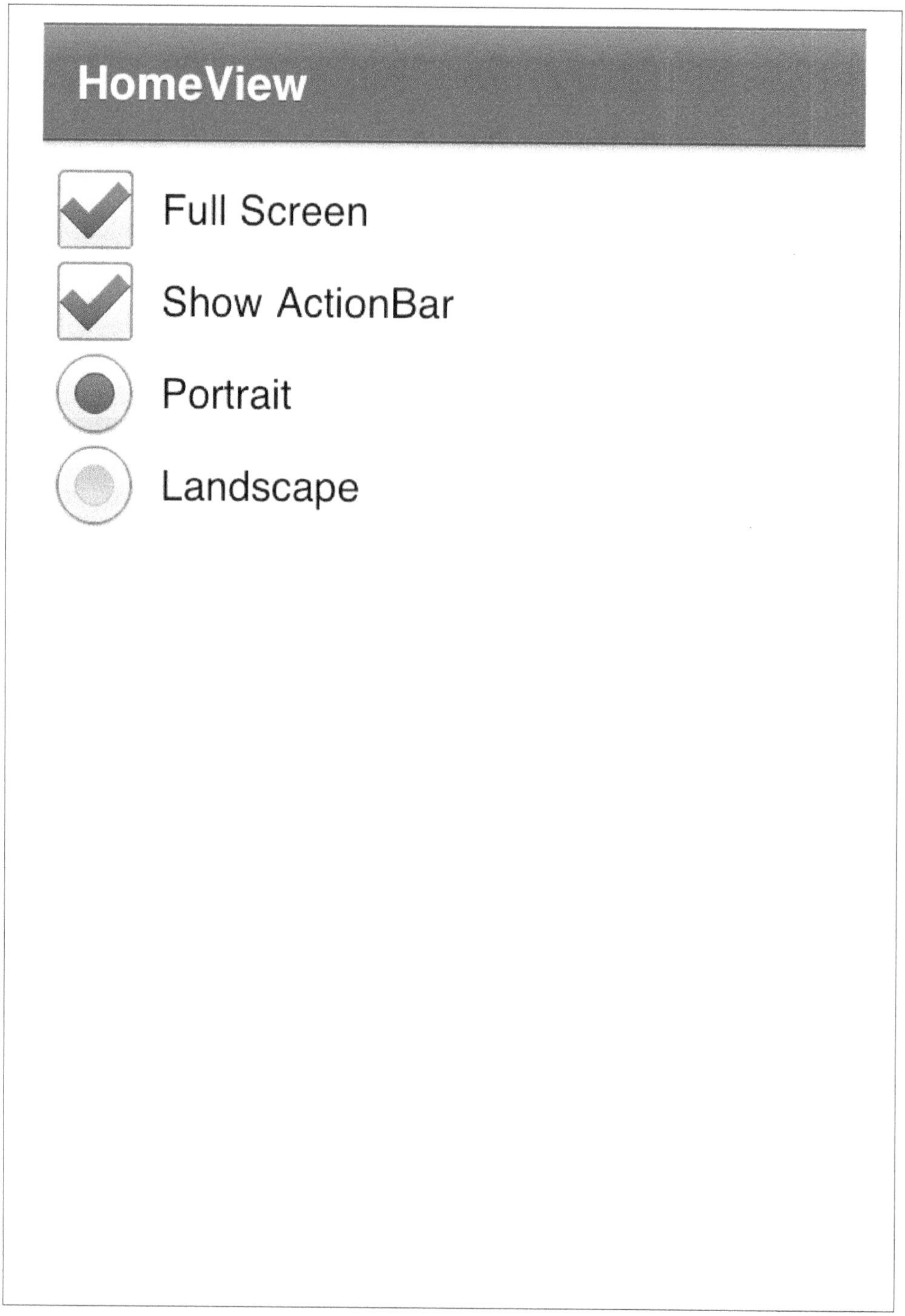

HomeView

 Full Screen

 Show ActionBar

 Portrait

 Landscape

Figure 6-15. Full Screen mode

ActionBar

The *ActionBar* is the built-in navigation that comes along with the view-based or tabbed application layouts. This bar does consume significant real estate on the screen. Therefore, the option to hide and show this bar programmatically is available to you as the developer.

The code below includes a `CheckBox` with the label "Show ActionBar". This `CheckBox` is set to selected by default, as that is the normal state of the `ActionBar`. When clicking on this `CheckBox` to check or uncheck the value, the `checkbox2_clickHandler` is called. The `actionBarVisible` of this `View` is set to the value of the `CheckBox`. The results can be seen in Figure 6-16, which shows an application in full screen mode, with the *Action-Bar* hidden:

```
<?xml version="1.0" encoding="utf-8"?>
<s:View xmlns:fx="http://ns.adobe.com/mxml/2009"
        xmlns:s="library://ns.adobe.com/flex/spark" title="HomeView">

    <fx:Script>
        <![CDATA[
            protected function checkbox1_clickHandler(event:MouseEvent):void
            {
                if(event.target.selected){
                  stage.displayState = StageDisplayState.FULL_SCREEN_INTERACTIVE;
                } else {
                    stage.displayState = StageDisplayState.NORMAL;
                }
            }

            protected function checkbox2_clickHandler(event:MouseEvent):void
            {
                this.actionBarVisible = event.target.selected;
            }

            protected function radiobutton1_clickHandler(event:MouseEvent):void
            {
                if(orientation.selectedValue == "portrait"){
                    stage.setAspectRatio(StageAspectRatio.PORTRAIT);
                } else if(orientation.selectedValue == "landscape"){
                    stage.setAspectRatio(StageAspectRatio.LANDSCAPE);
                }
            }

        ]]>
    </fx:Script>

    <fx:Declarations>
        <s:RadioButtonGroup id="orientation"/>
    </fx:Declarations>
```

```
<s:VGroup top="20" left="10">
    <s:CheckBox click="checkbox1_clickHandler(event)" label="Full Screen"/>
    <s:CheckBox click="checkbox2_clickHandler(event)" label="Show ActionBar"
            selected="true"/>
    <s:RadioButton groupName="orientation" value="portrait" label="Portrait"
                click="radiobutton1_clickHandler(event)" selected="true"/>
    <s:RadioButton groupName="orientation" value="landscape" label="Landscape"
                click="radiobutton1_clickHandler(event)"/>
</s:VGroup>


</s:View>
```

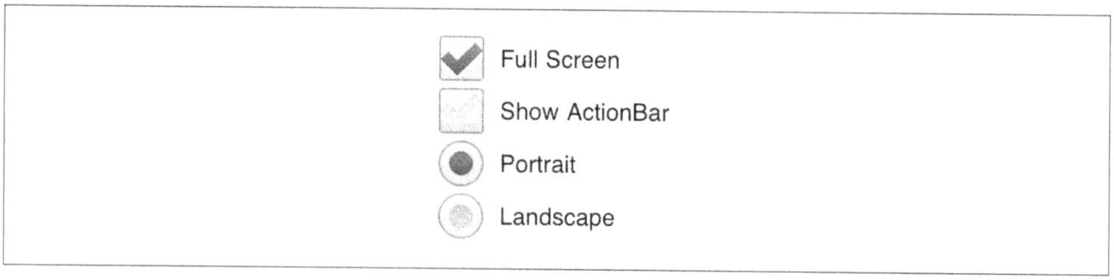

Figure 6-16. Full Screen mode with ActionBar hidden

CHAPTER 7

Designing for iOS

Anyone who has built a native iOS application knows that getting app store approval is not a trivial part of the project. Unlike the Android market, Apple reviews every application and will reject your application if it doesn't follow their guidelines. We can't go through all of these guidelines within the context of this book, but I can show you a few techniques so that you can maintain one version of your code and still target iOS with specific UI elements.

MultiDPIBitmap

The resolution of an iOS device varies depending on the device. The devices with higher resolutions have a greater DPI (pixel density). To allow your application images to display correctly across these resolutions, you can use *MultiDPIBitmapSource* to define multiple versions of your bitmaps and ensure that the appropriate bitmap is used. The example below defines 3 versions of an image. The first is 36×36 pixels in size, the second is 54×54 pixels, and the third is 72×72 pixels. If the operating system's DPI is less than 200 (like on the iPhone 3G), the 36×36 image will be used; if the DPI is greater than or equal to 200 and less than 280, the 54×54 will be used; and if the DPI is greater or equal to 280 (like on the iPhone 4), the 72×72 will be used. Figure 7-1 shows this application running on an iPhone 3 with a screen resolution of 320×480 (163 DPI), and Figure 7-2 shows this application running on an iPod with a screen resolution of 640×960 (326 DPI):

```
<?xml version="1.0" encoding="utf-8"?>
<s:Application xmlns:fx="http://ns.adobe.com/mxml/2009"
               xmlns:s="library://ns.adobe.com/flex/spark">
    <fx:Declarations>
        <!-- Place non-visual elements (e.g., services, value objects) here -->
    </fx:Declarations>
    <fx:Script>
        <![CDATA[
            import mx.core.FlexGlobals;
```

```
protected function button1_clickHandler(event:MouseEvent):void
{
    log.text = "Image: " +
        myImage.source.getSource(
            FlexGlobals.topLevelApplication.runtimeDPI)
        .toString() +
        "\nDPI: " + Capabilities.screenDPI +
        "\nResolution" +
        Capabilities.screenResolutionX + " x " +
        Capabilities.screenResolutionY;
}

]]>
</fx:Script>

<s:VGroup verticalCenter="0">
    <s:Image id="myImage">
        <s:source>
            <s:MultiDPIBitmapSource
                source160dpi="icons/logo36.png"
                source240dpi="icons/logo54.png"
                source320dpi="icons/logo72.png"/>
        </s:source>
    </s:Image>
    <s:Button label="getSource" click="button1_clickHandler(event)"/>
    <s:TextArea id="log"/>
</s:VGroup>
</s:Application>
```

Figure 7-1. A 36×36 image on iPhone 3

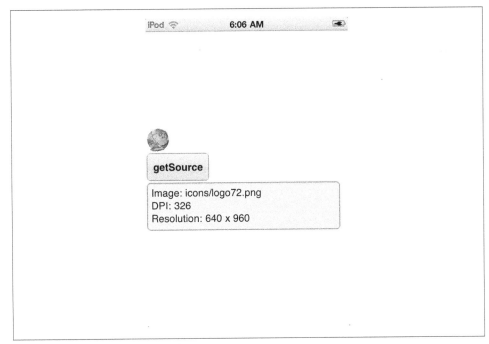

Figure 7-2. A 72×72 image on iPod

Setting Styles for iOS

CSS stylesheets are a great way for you to style your application; Adobe has provided the ability to use different CSS declarations according to rules defined in what is called the @media rule. Thanks to the ability to have conditional logic in your CSS using the @media rule, you can test for screen DPI or operating system. This makes it easy to style your application to meet the needs of any device.

The example below has some conditional logic to test for the application DPI as well as the operating system.

If the application DPI is less than 200, the Label font size will be set to 30 on all operating systems; if it is greater than or equal to 200 and less than 280, the font size will be set to 40; and if it is greater than or equal to 280, the font size will be set to 50.

There is also an operating system-specific CSS style defined for iOS devices. If the device is iOS, the *ActionBar*'s `defaultButtonAppearance` is set to beveled, which is the standard look on an iOS device.

The available values that you can test for with the `application-dpi` property are 160, 240, and 320. The available values that you can test for with the `os-platform` property are Android, iOS, Macintosh, Linux, QNX, and Windows.

 QNX is the BlackBerry Tablet operating system.

Using these properties, you can easily style your application to run on different operating systems and screen resolutions.

Figure 7-3 shows this application running on an iPhone 3, Figure 7-4 shows it on an iPod 4, and Figure 7-5 shows it on an Android phone.

Here is the code for the main application file:

```
<?xml version="1.0" encoding="utf-8"?>
<s:ViewNavigatorApplication xmlns:fx="http://ns.adobe.com/mxml/2009"
                             xmlns:s="library://ns.adobe.com/flex/spark"
    firstView="views.CSSSampleHomeView">
    <fx:Declarations>
        <!-- Place non-visual elements (e.g., services, value objects) here -->
    </fx:Declarations>

    <fx:Style>
        @namespace s "library://ns.adobe.com/flex/spark";
        @namespace mx "library://ns.adobe.com/flex/mx";

        /* dpi less than 200 */
        @media (application-dpi: 160) {
            s|Label {
                fontSize: 30;
            }
        }

        /* dpi greater than or equal to 200 and less than 280 */
        @media (application-dpi: 240) {
            s|Label {
                fontSize: 40;
            }
        }

        /* dpi greater than or equal to 280 */
        @media (application-dpi: 320) {
            s|Label {
                fontSize: 50;
            }
        }
```

```
        /* platform is iOS */
        @media(os-platform:"IOS")
        {
            s|ActionBar
            {
                defaultButtonAppearance:beveled;
            }

        }

    </fx:Style>


    <s:navigationContent>
        <s:Button label="Back"/>
    </s:navigationContent>

</s:ViewNavigatorApplication>
```

Code for the CSSSampleHomeView:

```
<?xml version="1.0" encoding="utf-8"?>
<s:View xmlns:fx="http://ns.adobe.com/mxml/2009"
        xmlns:s="library://ns.adobe.com/flex/spark" title="HomeView">
    <fx:Declarations>
        <!-- Place non-visual elements (e.g., services, value objects) here -->
    </fx:Declarations>


    <s:Label text="Hello World" horizontalCenter="0" verticalCenter="0"/>

</s:View>
```

Figure 7-3. The application on iPhone 3

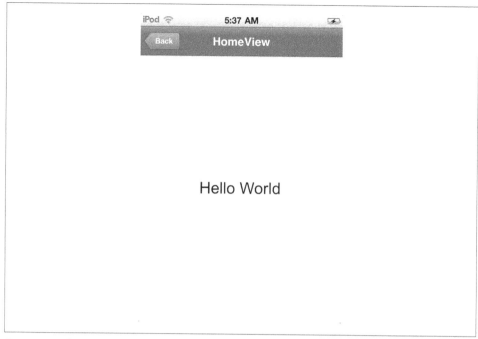

Figure 7-4. The application on iPod 4

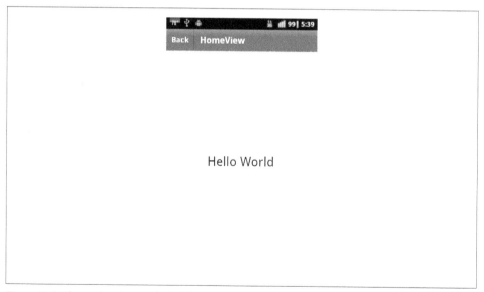

Figure 7-5. The application on Android

The @media rule also supports operators, so that you can apply a style only if multiple conditions are present.

The *and* operator is supported—for example:

This statement "*@media (os-platform: "IOS") and (application-dpi: 160)*" will only be true if the operating system is iOS and the screen DPI is less than 200.

The *or* operator is supported by using a comma—for example:

The statement "*@media (os-platform: "IOS"), (application-dpi: 160)*" will be true if the operating system is iOS or the screen DPI is less than 200.

The *not* operator is supported—for example:

The statement "*@media not all and (os-platform: "QNX")*" will be true for all operating systems except for QNX (BlackBerry Tablet OS).

Here is a sample:

```
<?xml version="1.0" encoding="utf-8"?>
<s:Application xmlns:fx="http://ns.adobe.com/mxml/2009"
               xmlns:s="library://ns.adobe.com/flex/spark">
    <fx:Declarations>
        <!-- Place non-visual elements (e.g., services, value objects) here -->
    </fx:Declarations>

    <fx:Style>
        @namespace s "library://ns.adobe.com/flex/spark";
        @namespace mx "library://ns.adobe.com/flex/mx";

        /*
            platform is iOS
            dpi greater than 280
        */
        @media (os-platform: "IOS") and (application-dpi: 320) {
            s|Label {
                fontSize: 100;
            }
        }

        /*
            platform is Android
            dpi greater than or equal to 200 and less than 280
        */
        @media (os-platform: "Android") and (application-dpi: 240) {
            s|Label {
                fontSize: 50;
            }
        }

        /*
            platform is iOS
            dpi is less than 200
            OR
            platform is Android
            dpi is less than 200
        */
```

```
@media (os-platform: "IOS") and (application-dpi:160),
        (os-platform: "ANDROID") and (application-dpi: 160) {
    s|Label {
        fontSize: 30;
    }
}

</fx:Style>


<s:Label text="Hello World"
        horizontalCenter="0" verticalCenter="0"/>

</s:Application>
```

Using Capabilities

So far you have seen how to use CSS to control some of the visual aspects of your application, but you may also wish to have only certain pieces of your application available to target specific devices or specific views created for specific devices. This is possible by utilizing the properties of the `Capabilities` class to determine operating system, screen resolution, and so on. The example below will serve a different home screen to the user depending on their device. This technique will allow you to target specific audiences with a custom experience. The `firstView` property of the `View NavigatorApplication` is bound to a function called `getFirstView`, which evaluates the `Capabilities.version`, and returns a different view based on the operating system (see Figures 7-6 and 7-7).

You could also use other properties of the `Capabilities` class in the same manner. You may wish to look into `Capabilities.screenDPI`, `Capabilities.screenResolutionX`, `Capabilities.screenResolutionY`, and `Capabilities.screenColor`:

 I could also have had just one main view file, and simply set the state of that file to be different based on the operating system.

```
<?xml version="1.0" encoding="utf-8"?>
<s:ViewNavigatorApplication xmlns:fx="http://ns.adobe.com/mxml/2009"
                            xmlns:s="library://ns.adobe.com/flex/spark"
                            firstView="{getFirstView(Capabilities.version)}">
    <fx:Declarations>
        <!-- Place non-visual elements (e.g., services, value objects) here -->
    </fx:Declarations>
    <fx:Script>
        <![CDATA[
            import views.*;
            private function getFirstView(v:String):Class{
```

```
                    if(v.indexOf("AND") == 0){
                        return views.AndroidHomeView;
                    } else if (v.indexOf("IOS") == 0){
                        return views.IOSHomeView;
                    }
                    return views.GenericHomeView;

                }

            ]]>
        </fx:Script>
</s:ViewNavigatorApplication>
```

Figure 7-6. View determined by Capabilities.version (Android)

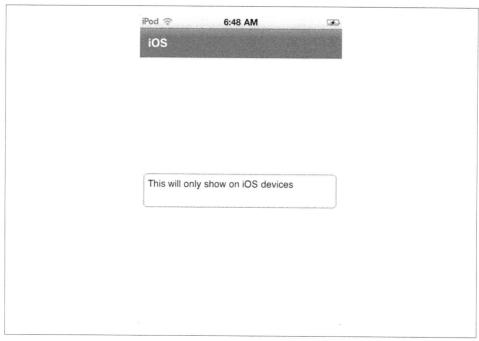

Figure 7-7. View determined by Capabilities.version (iOS)

CHAPTER 8

Publish to iOS Installer

Now that you have created your new application, it is time to publish it to an Apple iOS installer file, which is an archive file with the extension of *.ipa*. Flash Builder provides all of the tools to accomplish this task.

To demonstrate how to compile an application to an Apple iOS installer, let's walk through this process by following the following steps.

To add a custom icon for your application, you will need to add some image definitions to the icon block of the application descriptor XML file. The image sizes specific to iOS in the sample below are: 29×29, 57×57, 72×72, and 114×114. 57×57 and 114×114 are required for iPhone/iPod, 72×72 is required for iPad and it is also recommended to include a 29×29 version as well. The sample below shows these sizes, as well as some others that are required if you plan to compile to Android or BlackBerry:

 You will also need a 512×512 version of your application icon for the App Store.

```
<!-- The icon the system uses for the application.
    For at least one resolution,
    specify the path to a PNG file included
    in the AIR package. Optional. -->
<icon>
        <image16x16>icons/logo16.png</image16x16>
        <image29x29>icons/logo29.png</image29x29>
        <image32x32>icons/logo32.png</image32x32>
        <image36x36>icons/logo36.png</image36x36>
        <image48x48>icons/logo48.png</image48x48>
        <image57x57>icons/logo57.png</image57x57>
        <image72x72>icons/logo72.png</image72x72>
        <image114x114>icons/logo114.png</image114x114>
        <image128x128>icons/logo128.png</image128x128>
</icon>
```

First, click on File→Export within Flash Builder's main menu. See Figure 8-1.

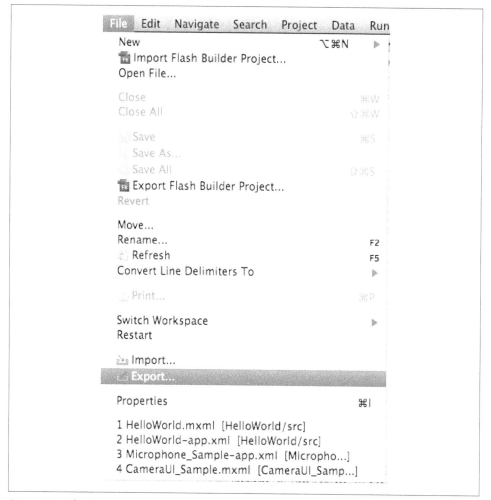

Figure 8-1. File→Export

Next, select Flash Builder→Release Build. See Figure 8-2.

Within the Export Release Build window, select the Project and Application that you would like to compile (Apple iOS). See Figure 8-3.

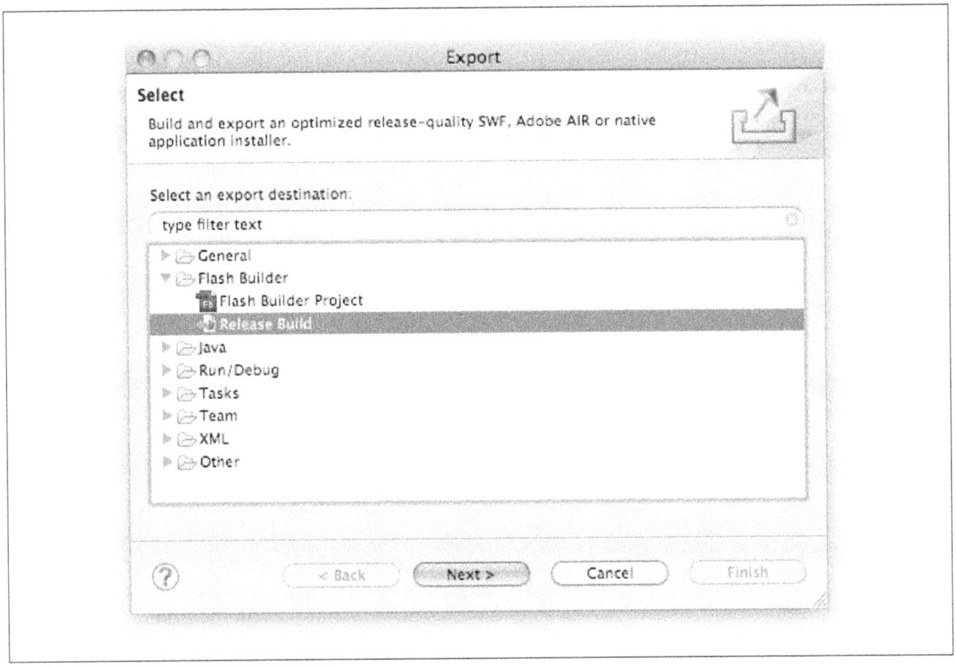

Figure 8-2. Flash Builder→Release Build

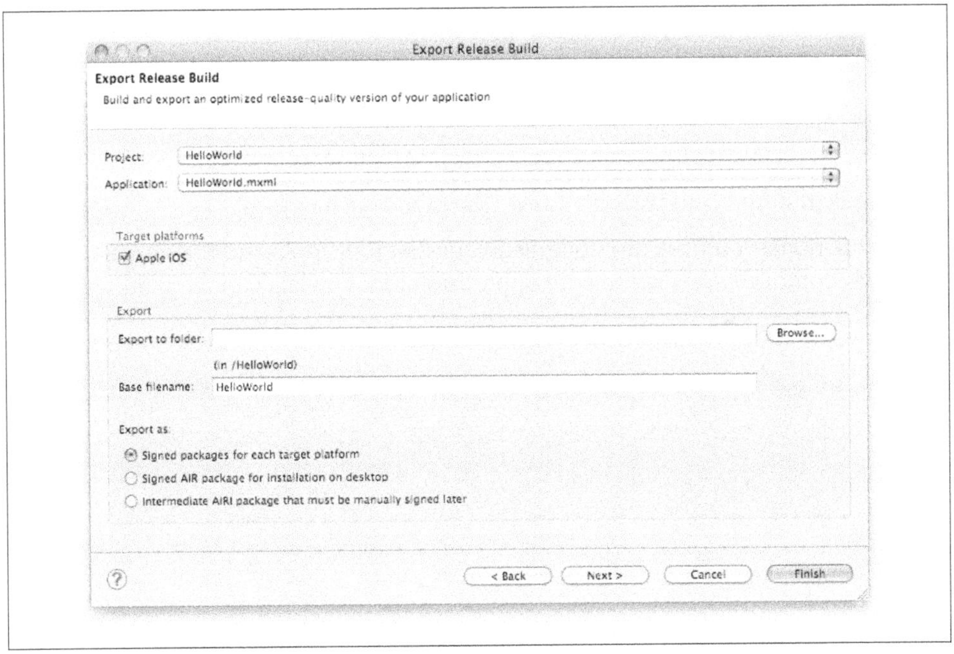

Figure 8-3. Export Release Build

You will need to go back to the iOS developer center and generate a distribution provisioning profile so that you can compile your application for the App Store. Once you have selected your distribution certificates, you can choose "Final release package for Apple App Store". Figure 8-4 shows an example of signing information.

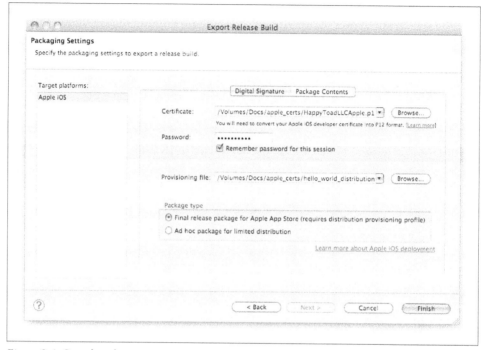

Figure 8-4. Complete the export

To compile the Apple installer file (*.ipa*), click the Finish button.

Congratulations, you have just compiled your first iOS application! Figure 8-5 shows the newly compiled application with application icons installed on an iPod.

Figure 8-5. Hello World installed on iPod

About the Author

Rich Tretola, an award-winning Flex developer, is the Applications Development Manager at Herff Jones Inc. He has been building Internet applications for over a decade, and has worked with Flex since the original Royale beta was introduced in 2003. Outside of Flex, Rich builds applications using ColdFusion, Flash, and Java. He is highly regarded in the Flex community as an expert in RIA, and is also a five-time Adobe Community Professional.

He is the lead author of Professional Flex 2 (Wrox) and sole author of Beginning AIR (Wrox). He is also a contributing author on Adobe AIR 1.5 Cookbook (O'Reilly), Flex 4 Cookbook (O'Reilly), Developing Android Applications with Flex 4.5 (O'Reilly), and Developing Blackberry Tablet Applications with Flex 4.5 (O'Reilly). He runs a popular Flex and AIR blog at EverythingFlex.com, was the community manager of Inside-RIA.com for over three years, and has also been a speaker at over 10 Adobe MAX sessions.

Recently, Rich has re-engaged the RIA development community by founding RIARockStars.com, and has been a principal partner in a new social polling service at twittapolls.com. For a non-technical escape, Rich is also a co-owner of a chocolate company in Hawaii named WowWee Maui (*http://www.wowweemaui.com*).

Get even more for your money.

Join the O'Reilly Community, and register the O'Reilly books you own. It's free, and you'll get:

- $4.99 ebook upgrade offer
- 40% upgrade offer on O'Reilly print books
- Membership discounts on books and events
- Free lifetime updates to ebooks and videos
- Multiple ebook formats, DRM FREE
- Participation in the O'Reilly community
- Newsletters
- Account management
- 100% Satisfaction Guarantee

Signing up is easy:

1. **Go to: oreilly.com/go/register**
2. **Create an O'Reilly login.**
3. **Provide your address.**
4. **Register your books.**

Note: English-language books only

To order books online:
oreilly.com/store

For questions about products or an order:
orders@oreilly.com

To sign up to get topic-specific email announcements and/or news about upcoming books, conferences, special offers, and new technologies:
elists@oreilly.com

For technical questions about book content:
booktech@oreilly.com

To submit new book proposals to our editors:
proposals@oreilly.com

O'Reilly books are available in multiple DRM-free ebook formats. For more information:
oreilly.com/ebooks

O'REILLY®

Spreading the knowledge of innovators   oreilly.com

©2010 O'Reilly Media, Inc. O'Reilly logo is a registered trademark of O'Reilly Media, Inc. 00000

The information you need, when and where you need it.

With Safari Books Online, you can:

Access the contents of thousands of technology and business books

- Quickly search over 7000 books and certification guides
- Download whole books or chapters in PDF format, at no extra cost, to print or read on the go
- Copy and paste code
- Save up to 35% on O'Reilly print books
- **New!** Access mobile-friendly books directly from cell phones and mobile devices

Stay up-to-date on emerging topics before the books are published

- Get on-demand access to evolving manuscripts.
- Interact directly with authors of upcoming books

Explore thousands of hours of video on technology and design topics

- Learn from expert video tutorials
- Watch and replay recorded conference sessions

Spreading the knowledge of innovators   safari.oreilly.com

©2009 O'Reilly Media, Inc. O'Reilly logo is a registered trademark of O'Reilly Media, Inc. 00000

Lightning Source UK Ltd.
Milton Keynes UK
UKHW031438170122
397284UK00005B/212

9 781449 308360